A CORD *Of* THREE STRANDS

A

CORD
Of THREE
STRANDS

Three Centuries of Christian Love Letters

DIANA LYNN SEVERANCE

Also available in e-book format.

Copyright © Diana Lynn Severance 2012

ISBN 978-1-84550-950-7

10 9 8 7 6 5 4 3 2 1

First published in 2012
by
Christian Focus Publications,
Geanies House, Fearn,
Ross-shire, IV20 1TW, Scotland
www.christianfocus.com

Cover design
by
Paul Lewis

Printed by
Bell and Bain, Glasgow

FOR GORDON

*Daily, and several times each day, I thank the Lord
for our cord of three strands.
Your love for me and our marriage
are indeed part of God's Amazing Grace.*

CONTENTS

MAPS

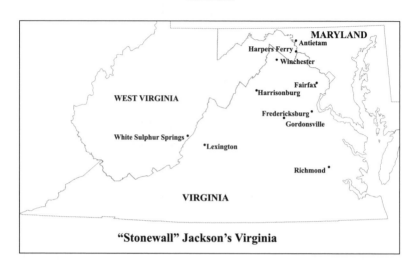

"Stonewall" Jackson's Virginia

**Places in Britain associated with
John Winthrop, Henry Martyn,
John Newton and Charles Spurgeon**

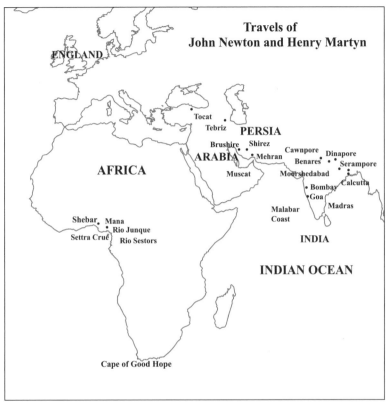

Travels of
John Newton and Henry Martyn

ENGLAND

Tocat
Tebriz
PERSIA
Brushire Shirez
ARABIA Mehran
Cawnpore Dinapore
Benares Serampore
AFRICA Muscat Moorshedabad
Calcutta
Bombay
Goa
Madras
Malabar
Coast

Shebar Mana
Rio Junque
Settra Cruc Rio Sestors
INDIA

INDIAN OCEAN

Cape of Good Hope

North Sea
Baltic Sea
Patzig
Buchenwalde
Finkenwalde
Berlin
Hannover

GERMANY

Flossenburg

FRANCE

Key Places in Bonhoeffer's Germany

PROLOGUE

In every age there have been exemplary marriages and betrothals held together by an indestructible bond. This book presents love letters of seven such couples, written over the course of three centuries, from three different continents, by people from very different stations and occupations in life. Yet amazingly, a distinct thread of common experience and thought can be seen running through these lovers' lives. This thread guaranteed for each couple a lasting, happy relationship that triumphed over daunting danger and crippling adversity. What is the difference between such enduring unions and the short-lived marriages that we so often see today?

Some might say the key is a courtship long enough for the parties to learn that they are compatible. Other armchair psychologists could propose that strong will-power alone can bind a union together against the onslaughts of adversity. Curiously, Solomon, famous for his wisdom, provides another explanation. As he looked back on all of his life's experiences, he wrote:

Two are better than one
Because they have a good return for their labor.

For if either of them falls, the one will lift up his companion.
But woe to the one who falls when there is not another to lift
    him up.
Furthermore, if two lie down together, they keep warm,
But how can one be warm alone?
And if one can overpower him who is alone, two can resist him.
A cord of three strands is not quickly torn apart.
(Eccles. 4:9-12, NASB)

In this discourse, Solomon talks about the advantages of *two*
together, then suddenly he is talking about *three*. Why the change?
And what and where is the third strand? The seven couples whose
love letters appear in this book all entered into their relationship
with the firm conviction that if their betrothal and marriage were
interwoven with Jesus Christ, then their marriage would have
a depth, strength and stability unknown to the world. For them,
faith in the Trinity – God, Christ, and the indwelling Holy Spirit-
-was the third strand! They all prayed for God to guide their
decision for betrothal and marriage. Most of the couples faced
daunting trials and tribulation seldom encountered in world
history. For all of them, the cord of three strands held firm—in
life, in death, for eternity.

These seven couples all experienced a love of incredible,
enduring depth and beauty. All of them had a solemn
commitment to obey Christ's command, to trust Him in the
face of life-threatening adversity. They all had discovered the
same secret: that saving faith in Christ not only restored the
individual's fellowship with God, but also could weld the
marriage relationship into a single, inseparable unit.

In their day, the seven couples whose letters follow all played
very public roles on the world's stage:

Public servants: General Thomas 'Stonewall' Jackson   &   Mary Anna
                         (Confederate military leader during
                         the American Civil War)

	John Winthrop	&	Margaret
	(Founder and first governor of the Massachusetts Bay Colony)		
<u>Martyrs who died because of their faith:</u>	Dietrich Bonhoeffer	&	Maria
	(Theologian executed by the Nazis at the end of World War II)		
	Henry Martyn	&	Lydia
	(Missionary to India and Persia)		
	Christopher Love	&	Mary
	(Pastor executed during the English Civil War)		
<u>Pastors:</u>	John Newton	&	Mary
	(Slave trader and author of 'Amazing Grace')		
	Charles Spurgeon	&	Susannah
	(Leading preacher in Victorian England)		

In each case, the bond of love between these heroes and heroines was strengthened, enlarged, and elevated to unimaginable heights—by simple faith and trust in Jesus as savior, friend, and guide. As the faith of each grew, each experienced the assurance that the closeness of the relationship would endure into eternity. Such a view of romantic love is unknown to those in the world who have closed their minds to faith. The secret to experiencing the wonder, exhilaration, permanence, *and the heavenly source* of such love was poignantly revealed in the classic historical novel *Quo Vadis*. After the hero, Vinicius, became a Christian during Nero's persecutions and married the Christian Lygia, he wrote to his Roman friend:

> I am happy…[and] my happiness is Lygia…because I love her immortal soul, and because we both love each other in Christ; for such love there is no separation, no deceit, no change, no old age, no death. For, when youth and beauty pass, when our

bodies wither and death comes, love will remain, for the spirit remains.[1]

Even though the correspondence of these fourteen Christian men and women was written from three continents over three centuries, the love expressed by these writers reflects amazing uniformity in their views of marriage, their religious and moral conviction, and their qualities of character. These letters contain many examples of their shared Christian values. As the depth of the writers' character becomes increasingly apparent, at some point, we may even ask ourselves, 'Are there any lessons we can learn for our own lives from these very personal letters written so long ago?'

If we listen carefully, we can hear the lessons they are teaching, core principles of betrothal and marriage that we too can be willing to live by—and to die by! These principles are found in God's Word, the Holy Bible, which all of these couples read regularly. If we too depend on God and follow these principles, we too can have a love as strong and enduring as theirs!

1. **Love for God is most important.** Important as marriage is, love for our spouse should never become the controlling focal point in our lives. A love with all your heart, mind, soul, and strength is due only to God, not to any human being. ('You shall love the Lord your God with all your heart, with all your soul, and with all your strength.' [Deut. 6:5]) Many marriages have unraveled because they sought to find a paradise of love apart from God. A marriage that does not seek God first cannot bring fulfillment or true happiness. Total trust and security can only be found in God, not in any human relationship—even that of marriage. A Christian marriage must be rooted and grounded in the love of Christ. ('We know that we are of God, and the whole world lies *under the sway of* the wicked one. And we know that the Son of God has come, and has given us an understanding,

---

1   Henry Sienkiewicz (trans. Jeremiah Curtin), *Quo Vadis*. New York: Bantam Books, 1960, pp. 487-8.

that we may know Him who is true, and we are in Him who is true, in His Son Jesus Christ. This is the true God and eternal life' [1 John 5:19-20. See also Deut. 6:5; Exod. 20:3]).

2. You should live your life for eternity, not for riches or things of this world. Because our heart and focus is on the Lord and His heavenly, eternal truth, the things of this world lack attraction or power for us. Because of this focus on things eternal, hardships and difficulties never become major problems. They are recognized as tools in the Lord's hands to mold you after His will. If you always seek an eternal perspective in events, your trust in the Lord will never waver, and disasters can't upset or dampen your love. ('Do not lay up for yourselves treasures on earth, where moth and rust destroy, and where thieves break in and steal; but lay up for yourselves treasures in heaven, where neither moth nor rust destroys and where thieves do not break in or steal.' [Matt. 6:19-20]; 'Eye has not seen, nor ear heard, nor have entered into the heart of man, the things which God has prepared for those who love Him' [1 Cor. 2:9; see also Luke 14:15-33; Job 1:20]).

3. Love, especially marital love, is a special gift from God. God's providential care is like an umbrella covering everything in our lives. Nothing happens without His planning, provision, and protection. Because of this, you should be particularly thankful to Him in all things. Each day, God's gift of this special love should make you want to trust and serve Him more. His gift of love motivates you to stronger, more effective service for Him. ('In this is love, not that we loved God, but that He loved us and sent His Son to be the propitiation for our sins.' [1 John 4:10]; 'We love Him because He first loved us.' [1 John 4:19]; 'What then shall we say to these things? If God is for us, who can be against us? He who did not spare His own Son, but delivered Him up for us all, how shall He not also with Him freely give us all things? Who shall bring a charge against God's elect? It is God who justifies. Who is he who condemns? It is Christ Jesus who died, and furthermore is also risen, who is even at the right hand of God, who also makes intercession for us. Who shall separate us from the love of Christ? Shall tribulation, or distress, or persecution, or famine, or nakedness, or peril, or sword? As it is written, "For Your sake we are killed all day long: we are accounted as sheep for the slaughter." Yet in all these things we are more than conquerors through Him who loved us. For I am persuaded that neither death nor life, nor angels, nor principalities, nor powers, nor things present nor things to come, nor powers, nor height, nor depth, nor any other created thing, shall be able to separate us from the love of God, which is in Christ Jesus our Lord' [Rom. 8:31-39]; 'Or do you not know that your body is the temple of the Holy Spirit who is in you, whom you have from God, and that you are not your own? For you have been bought with a price: therefore glorify God in your body' [1 Cor. 6:19-20]. 'For the eyes of the Lord move to and fro throughout the earth, to show Himself strong on behalf of those whose heart is loyal to Him' [2 Chron. 16:9; see also James 1:17-18]).

4. Christian marital love is more interested in the other person than in satisfying personal needs or demanding personal rights and fulfillment. Rather than a selfish, inward-looking love, Christian marital love is selfless. Each partner is intensely interested in the spiritual development and progress of the other beloved partner. Each prays for the other's spiritual growth and physical well-being. Praying together, going to the throne of grace together, is one of the strongest ways marriage partners are bonded together with the cord of Christ's love—making them *a cord of three strands*. ('Husbands...dwell with them [your wives] with understanding, giving honor to the wife...as being heirs together of the grace of life, so that your prayers may not be hindered.' [1 Pet. 3:7]; 'So husbands ought to love their own wives as their own bodies: he who loves his own wife loves himself' [Eph. 5:28]).

5. Christian love is very humble. Neither partner in the engagement or marriage considers himself or herself worthy of the other. Each considers the other to be the better partner. This attitude fosters in each partner a continuous, innate sense of being honored that the other partner could love such an unworthy person. A deep gratitude at being so honored inspires each partner to exert a best effort to show a deep appreciation for such honor. One manifestation of this mutual appreciation is that the partners never tire of expressing their love, even with a simple, beautiful: 'I love you.' This attitude of humility is inextricably related to the attitude of each wanting to serve the other (cf. Item 4 above: 'For … I say to everyone who is among you, not to think more highly of himself that he ought to think…' [Rom. 12:3]; 'Love suffers long, and is kind; love does not envy; love does not parade itself, is not puffed up; does not behave rudely, does not seek its own, is not provoked, thinks no evil, does not rejoice in iniquity, but rejoices in the truth; bears all things, believes all things, hopes all things, endures all things. Love never fails…And now abide faith, hope, love, these three; but the greatest of these is love.' [1 Cor. 13:4-8, 13]; 'Let this mind be in you which was also in Christ Jesus' [Phil. 2:5; cf. Matt. 5:3-10]).

6. Love is centered in Christ; He is the third strand that provides strength for the marriage. Jesus Christ Himself brings a new creation, and *in Christ* individual souls as well as personal relationships are restored from the effects of sin and disharmony brought by the Fall. The harmony of marriage as originally created can be achieved by Christians *in Christ*. ('…if anyone is in Christ, he is a new creation; old things have passed away…all things have become new.' [2 Cor. 5:17; see also Eccles. 4:9-12; Gen. 1:26-27; 2:18-25; 3:16]).

It is unlikely that the couples whose letters you are about to read ever contemplated sharing their secret, most intimate sentiments with anyone other than their beloved. Yet the fact that their letters survived the centuries is Providential. To us in this secular twenty-first century, when the institution of marriage is under attack as never before, when half of the marriages end in divorce, these letters bring a special message of hope and examples of Christian marriage bonded together in Christ.

As we read about these seven betrothals and marriages, we see them holding together against the fury of the most devastating forces imaginable. When seven relationships stand fast against the daunting fury of war, lethal disease, imprisonment, or even execution, there are lessons to be learned from studying them. And it's just possible that these lessons may add yet one more couple to the list of marriages that are described as 'made in heaven!'

A Note on Transcription of the Letters

In transcribing the letters for this volume, the grammar, capitalization, and spelling of the originals were maintained, keeping the flavor of the originals as much as possible. A major exception were the Winthrop letters, whose archaic spelling was routinely modernized for ease in reading. Readers will notice some distinctive changes in grammar over the centuries. In earlier days, pronouns referring to God or Jesus were not routinely capitalized. Words such as 'to-day' and 'to-morrow' were hyphenated. References to other people were sometimes written as 'Mr /Mrs _____' with simply the first initial of the person's name given, the writer knowing the reader would know the person meant. When the identity of the person is known today, it has been given in the footnotes of the transcription.

THOMAS JONATHAN JACKSON
AND
MARY ANNA JACKSON

(1824-1863)   (1831-1915)

'...*my desire is to live <u>entirely</u> <u>and</u> <u>unconditionally</u> to God's glory.*
Pray, my darling, that I may so live.'
Thomas Jonathan Jackson

Thomas Jonathan 'Stonewall' Jackson was among the most brilliant of American soldiers. He was also a deeply committed Christian. A native of Virginia, both Jackson's father and his mother died by the time he was eight; he was brought up by aunts and uncles. In 1842 he entered West Point, where a poor boy could receive an education at government expense. Though he began at the bottom of his class, his hard work and dogged determination brought steady improvement. By the time he graduated, he was seventeenth in his class, with some observers remarking that if the course had been a year longer, he would have graduated first!

Jackson completed his West Point training in 1846, just as the war with Mexico began; here he saw his first military action. Here he was also challenged by Col. Francis Taylor to examine the Christian faith. Jackson began reading the Bible and systematically examining various Christian denominations, beginning with the Catholics in Mexico.

After the war he was stationed at Fort Hamilton in New York, where he accepted Jesus Christ as Savior and Redeemer and was baptized in the Episcopal Church. In 1851 he became professor of artillery tactics and natural philosophy at the Virginia Military Institute in Lexington, VA. There he attended several churches before joining the Presbyterian Church pastored by Dr William S. White. Jackson's Christian faith became the most absorbing part of his life. Not wishing to be conformed to the world, Jackson's Christian conscience kept him from amusements which he felt would lead him away from the things of God. Prayer became as constant as breathing. He accompanied even trivial acts with a silent prayer – when he drank a glass of water, he would thank God for his gifts; when he posted a letter, he always asked God's blessing on the recipient.

On August 4, 1853, Jackson married Elinor Junkin, daughter of Dr George Junkin, president of Washington College, also located in Lexington, Virginia. In October of the following year, Ellie delivered a stillborn daughter and died shortly thereafter. Jackson was devastated, and his friends feared for his sanity. Ellie's mother had died only seven months before, and the grieving Dr Junkin was able to comfort Tom in his own sorrow. In Dr Junkin, Jackson found the father he never had. Jackson was finally able to accept the death of his young wife and child. In a notebook he wrote:

> Objects to be effected by Ellie's death :
> To eradicate ambition; to eradicate resentment; to produce humility. If you desire to be more heavenly-minded, think more of the things of heaven, and less of the things of earth.

During this time the truths of Romans 8:28 became very real to Jackson, and he took that as his 'life verse'.

In 1856 Jackson took a three month tour of Europe. When he returned, he wrote to Mary Anna Morrison of North Carolina, whom he had met the summer of 1853 while she was visiting her sister, Mrs D. H. Hill, in Lexington. Anna was the daughter (fourth child of twelve!) of Presbyterian minister Rev. Dr Robert Morrison. Jackson soon followed up his letter with a visit. Anna's father was pleased that Jackson was a 'Christian gentleman,' while her mother was pleased by his extreme politeness. Thomas and Anna soon became engaged. Jackson's letters to his betrothed during their engagement reveal the Christian foundation of their love:[1]

> April 25th, 1857. It is a great comfort to me to know that although I am not with you, yet you are in the hands of One who will not permit any evil to come nigh you. What a consoling thought it is to know that we may, with perfect confidence, commit all our friends in Jesus to the care of our Heavenly Father, with an assurance that all will be well with them! ... I have been sorely disappointed at not hearing from you this morning, but these disappointments are all designed for our good.
>
> In my daily walks I think much of you. I love to stroll abroad after the labors of the day are over, and indulge feelings of gratitude to God for all the sources of natural beauty with which he has adorned the earth. Some time since, my morning walks were rendered very delightful by the singing of the birds. The morning caroling of the birds, and their sweet notes in the evening, awaken in me devotional feelings of praise and thanksgiving, though very different in their nature. In the morning, all animated nature (man excepted) appears to join in expressions of gratitude to God; in the evening, all is hushing into silent slumber, and this disposes the mind to meditation. And as my mind dwells on you, I love to give it a devotional turn, by thinking of you as a gift from our Heavenly Father. How delightful it is thus to associate every pleasure and enjoyment with God the Giver! Thus will He bless us, and make us grow in grace, and in the knowledge of Him, whom to know aright is life eternal.

---

1   Thomas Jackson's letters are taken from Mary Anna Jackson's *Memoirs of 'Stonewall' Jackson*. Louisville, Kentucky: Courier-Journal Job Printing Co., 1895.

May 7th. I wish I could be with you to-morrow at your communion. Though absent in body, yet in spirit I shall be present, and my prayer will be for your growth in every Christian grace ... I take special pleasure in the part of my prayers in which I beg that every temporal and spiritual blessing may be yours, and that the glory of God may be the controlling and absorbing thought of our lives in our new relation. It is to me a great satisfaction to feel that our Heavenly Father has so manifestly ordered our union. I believe, and am persuaded, that if we but walk in His commandments, acknowledging Him in all our ways, He will shower His blessings upon us. How delightful it is to feel that we have such a friend, who changes not! The Christian's recognition of God in all His works greatly enhances his enjoyment.

May 16th. There is something very pleasant in the thought of your mailing me a letter every Monday; such manifestation of regard for the Sabbath must be well-pleasing in the sight of God. Oh that all our people would manifest such a regard for his holy day! If we would all strictly observe his holy laws, what would not our country be? ... When in prayer for you last Sabbath, the tears came to my eyes, and I realized an unusual degree of emotional tenderness. I have not yet fully analyzed my feelings to my satisfaction, so as to arrive at the cause of such emotions; but I am disposed to think that it consisted in the idea of the intimate relation existing between you, as the object of my tender affection, and God, to whom I looked up as my Heavenly Father. I felt that day as if it were a communion day for myself. ...

June 20th. I never remember to have felt so touchingly as last Sabbath the pleasure springing from the thought of prayers ascending for my welfare from one tenderly beloved. There is something very delightful in such spiritual communion.

Thomas and Anna were married at Anna's North Carolina home on July 16, 1857. After a northern tour to Niagara and Saratoga, the newlyweds settled in Lexington. In November of 1858, they bought a house which they made full of domestic Christian love. They enjoyed working in their garden together and riding into the countryside or reading in the evenings. As deacon in the Presbyterian Church, Jackson was especially interested in the slaves and taught a Negro Sunday School class.

In the summers, Anna and Tom would often go north to cooler weather and enjoy the mineral springs then considered so healthful. Sorrow came in May, 1858, when their month-old daughter Mary Graham died of jaundice. Anna herself was not well the following year, and in the spring Jackson took her to New York for treatment. He had to leave her there for a time while he returned to his teaching:

> March, 1859. I got home last night in as good health as when I gave my darling the last kiss. Hetty and Amy[2] came to the door when I rang, but would not open until I gave my name. They made much ado about my not bringing you home. Your husband has a sad heart. Our house looks so deserted without my *esposa*.[3] Home is not home without my little dove. I love to talk to you, little one, as though you were here, and tell you how much I love you, but that will not give you the news ... During our absence the servants appear to have been faithful, and I am well pleased with the manner in which they discharged their duties. George came to me to-day, saying he had filled all the wood-boxes and asked permission to go fishing, which was granted. ... You must be cheerful and happy, remembering that you are somebody's sunshine.

---

2   Hetty and Amy were two of Jackson's servants (slaves). Hetty had been Anna's nursemaid when she was a baby; Hetty and her two boys came with Anna to Lexington. Amy was an old woman who begged Jackson to buy her when she was about to be sold for debt. She remained ever faithful to Jackson and was his cook and housekeeper.

3   Jackson had become familiar with Spanish while in Mexico during the war with that country. He often used Spanish terms of endearment in his letters. *Esposa* means 'wife'; sometimes he used *esposita*, meaning 'little wife'. *Esposo* means 'husband.'

May 7th. I received only three letters last week, and have only one so far this week, but 'hope springs eternal in the human breast;' so you see I am becoming quite poetical since listening to a lecture on the subject last evening ... I send you a flower from your garden, and could have sent one in full bloom, but I thought this one, which is just opening, would be in a better state of preservation when my little dove receives it. You must not give yourself any concern about your *esposo's* living. ... My little pet, your husband was made very happy at receiving two letters from you and learning that you were improving so rapidly. I have more than once bowed down on my knees, and thanked our kind and merciful Heavenly Father for the prospect of restoring you to health again. Now, don't get impatient, and come off before you are entirely well. ... Yesterday Doctor Junkin preached one of his masterly sermons on the sovereignty of God, and, although a doctrinal discourse, it was eminently consoling; and I wish that you could have heard such a presentation of the subject. To-day I rode your horse out to your lot and saw your laborers. They are doing good work. I was mistaken about your large garden fruit being peaches, they turn out to be apricots; and just think - my little woman has a tree full of them! You must come home before they get ripe. You have the greatest show of flowers I have seen this year. Enclosed are a few specimens. Our potatoes are coming up. We have had very uncommonly dry weather for nearly a fortnight, and your garden had been thirsting for rain till last evening, when the weather commenced changing, and to-day we have had some rain. Through grace given me from above, I felt that the rain would come at the right time, and I don't recollect having ever felt so grateful for rain as for the present one. ... You must not be discouraged at the slowness of recovery. Look up to Him who giveth liberally for faith to be resigned to His divine will, and trust Him for that measure of health which will most glorify Him and advance to the greatest extent your own real happiness. We are sometimes suffered to be in a state of perplexity, that our faith may be tried and grow stronger. 'All things work together for good' to God's children.[4] See if you cannot spend a short time after dark in looking out of your window into space, and meditating upon heaven, with all its joys unspeakable and full of glory; and think of what the Savior relinquished in glory when he came to earth, and of his sufferings for us, and seek to realize, with the apostle, that the afflictions of the present life are not worthy to be compared with the glory which shall be revealed in us. Try to look up and be cheerful, and not desponding. Trust our kind Heavenly Father, and by the eye of faith see that all things with you are right and for your best interest. The clouds come, pass over us, and are followed by bright sunshine; so in God's moral dealings with us, he permits us to have trouble awhile. But let us, even in the most trying dispensations of His providence, be cheered by the brightness which is a little ahead. Try to live near to Jesus, and secure that peace which flows like a river. You have your husband's prayers, sympathy, and love. ...

I am so glad and thankful that you received the draft and letters in time. How kind is God to his children! I feel so thankful that He has blessed me with so much faith, though I well know that I have not that faith which it is my privilege to have.[5] But I have been taught never to despair, but to wait, expecting the blessing at the last moment. Such occurrences should strengthen our faith in Him who never slumbers. ... I trust that our Heavenly Father is restoring my darling to health, and that when she gets home she will again be its sunshine. Your husband is looking forward with great joy to seeing her bright little face in her own home once more. If

---

4   Romans 8:28 was one of Jackson's favorite Bible passages, and he quoted it frequently.

5   Jackson is thankful for the faith he has, but realizes that with the privileges he has in Christ, it could be much stronger.

25

you should be detained longer, I will send you some summer clothing, but get everything that is necessary there. I sent you a check in order that you may have ample funds. I know how embarrassing it is even to anticipate scarcity of money when one is away from home. You are one darling of darlings, and may our kind and merciful Heavenly Father bless you with speedy restoration to health and to me, and with every needful blessing, both temporal and spiritual, is my oft-repeated prayer. ... On Wednesday your *esposo* hopes to meet his sunshine, and may he never see its brightness obscured, nor its brilliancy diminished by spots!

In the summer of 1859, Jackson went to White Sulphur Springs for two weeks for his health. He feared the stage-coach travel would be too tiring for Anna, so she stayed at the Rockbridge Baths. From White Sulphur Springs, Tom wrote Anna:

August 15th. Last night I enjoyed what I have long desired - listening to a sermon from the Rev. Dr. Thornwell,[6] of South Carolina. He opened with an introduction, setting forth the encouragements and discouragements under which he spoke. Among the encouragements, he stated that the good effected here would be widely disseminated, as there were visitors from every Southern State. Following the example of the apostle Paul, he observed that whilst he felt an interest in all, yet he felt a special interest in those from his own State.[7] He spoke of the educated and accomplished audience it was his privilege to address. After concluding his introductory remarks, he took his text from Genesis, seventeenth chapter, seventh verse, which he presented in a bold, profound, and to me original manner. I felt what a privilege it was to listen to such an exposition of God's truth. He showed that in

---

6   James Henley Thornwell (1812-1862) was a brilliant preacher and champion of orthodoxy against liberalism. He was probably the most influential Southern minister of his day.

7   Romans 1:16.

Adam's fall we had been raised from the position of servants to that of children of God. He gave a brief account of his own difficulties when a college student, in comprehending his relation to God. He represented man as a redeemed being at the day of judgment, standing nearest to the throne, the angels being farther removed. And why? Because *his Brother* is sitting upon the throne he is a nearer relation to Christ than the angels. And his righteousness is superior to that of the angels - his being the righteousness of God himself. I don't recollect having ever before felt such love to God. I was rather surprised at seeing so much grace and gesture in Dr. Thornwell. I hope and pray that much good will result from this great exposition of Bible truth. ... Early yesterday morning the tables in the parlor were well supplied with religious tracts. ... Time passes more pleasantly here than I expected, but I want to get back to my *esposita*, and I never want to go to any watering-place without her again.

In the fall of 1859 John Brown led his raid on the U.S. military arsenal at Harper's Ferry, Virginia, hoping to encourage a revolt of the slaves against their Southern masters. He was arrested on charges of treason, tried, convicted, and condemned to execution. Governor Wise of Virginia feared an attempt would be made to rescue Brown and ordered troops to insure peace. Major Jackson marched the corps of cadets of V.M.I. to serve as guards at the execution.

With the growing discord in the country, Jackson foresaw the coming of war. Knowing war's horrors, he deprecated war while radicals on both sides clamored for it. Jackson earnestly spoke to his pastor about the need for Christian people to unite in a concert of prayer to avert war from their land. On April 21, 1861, Major Jackson received his orders at Lexington to <u>immediately</u> bring the V.M.I. cadets to Richmond. On that day, he left his home, full of domestic happiness, never to return again. Jackson wrote Anna almost daily concerning his military activities and the progress of the war.

Winchester, April 27th [1861]

I came from Richmond yesterday, and expect to leave here about half-past two o'clock this afternoon for Harper's Ferry. On last Saturday the Governor handed me my commission as Colonel of Virginia Volunteers, the post which I prefer above all others, and has given me an independent command. Little one, you must not expect to hear from me very often, as I expect to have more work than I have ever had in the same length of time before but don't be concerned about your husband, for our kind Heavenly Father will give every needful aid.

[July]. I have been officially informed of my promotion to be a brigadier-general of the Provisional Army of the Southern Confederacy, but it was prior to my skirmish with the enemy.[8] My letter from the Secretary of War was dated 17th of June. Thinking it would be gratifying to you, I send the letters of Generals Lee and Johnston. My promotion was beyond what I anticipated, as I only expected it to be in the voluntary forces of the State. One of my greatest desires for advancement is the gratification it will give my darling, and [the opportunity] of serving my country more efficiently. I have had all that I ought to desire in the line of promotion. I should be very ungrateful if I were not contented, and exceedingly thankful to our kind Heavenly Father. May his blessing ever rest on you is my fervent prayer. Try to live near to Jesus, and secure that peace which flows like a river.

Manassas, July 22ND

My precious Pet, - Yesterday we fought a great battle and gained a great victory, for which all the glory is due to *God alone*. Although under a heavy fire for several continuous hours, I received only one wound, the breaking of the longest finger of my left hand; but the doctor says the finger can be saved. It was broken about midway between the hand and knuckle, the ball passing on the side next the forefinger. Had

---

8   "Falling Waters' on July 2, 1861.

it struck the centre, I should have lost the finger. My horse was wounded, but not killed. Your coat got an ugly wound near the hip, but my servant, who is very handy, has so far repaired it that it doesn't show very much. My preservation was entirely due, as was the glorious victory, to our God, to whom be all the honor, praise, and glory. The battle was the hardest that I have ever been in, but not near so hot in its fire. I commanded the centre more particularly, though one of my regiments extended to the right for some distance. There were other commanders on my right and left. Whilst great credit is due to other parts of our gallant army, God made my brigade more instrumental than any other in repulsing the main attack.[9] This is for your information only-say nothing about it. Let others speak praise, not myself.

August 5th. And so you think the papers ought to say more about your husband! My brigade is not a brigade of newspaper correspondents. I know that the First Brigade was the first to meet and pass our retreating foes - to push on with no other aid than the smiles of God; to boldly take its position with the artillery that was under my command - to arrest the victorious foe in his onward progress - to hold him in check until reinforcements arrived - and finally to charge bayonets, and, thus advancing, pierce the enemy's centre. I am well satisfied with what it did, and so are my generals, Johnston and Beauregard. It is not to be expected that I should receive the credit that Generals Beauregard and Johnston would, because I was under them; but I am thankful to my ever-kind Heavenly Father that He makes me content to await His own good time and pleasure for commendation - knowing that all things work together for

---

9   During the first major battle of the Civil War, the Battle of First Manassas or First Bull Run, Federal reinforcements were causing the Confederates to fall back, but Jackson's brigade firmly held the center. Brigadier General Barnard Bee saw Jackson's troops holding firm and called to his men, 'There stands Jackson like a stone wall! Rally behind the Virginians!' Defeat was turned to victory as the Confederates charged until the Federals began a disorderly retreat to Washington, D.C. It was this incident that gave Jackson the nickname 'Stonewall,' though he always contended the title belonged to his brigade more than to him.

my good. If my brigade can always play so important and useful a part as it did in the last battle, I trust I shall ever be most grateful. As you think the papers do not notice me enough, I send a specimen, which you will see from the upper part of the paper is a leader. My darling, never distrust our God, who doeth all things well. In due time He will make manifest all His pleasure, which is all His people should desire. You must not be concerned at seeing other parts of the army lauded, and my brigade not mentioned. 'Truth is mighty and will prevail. ...'

In September, 1861, Anna was able to visit Jackson for two weeks near Fairfax, Virginia. It was the first of three visits to her husband she was able to make during the war. When she left Fairfax, Anna returned to Cottage Home, her parents' home in North Carolina. She had boarded up her Lexington home and stayed with her parents while Jackson was at war.

September 24th [1861]. I am going to write a letter to my darling pet *esposita*, who paid me such a sweet visit, and whose dear face I can still see, though she is 'way down in the Old North State. If my darling were here, I know she would enjoy General Jones's band, which plays very sweetly. We are still in the encampment as when you left, and I have the promise of three more wall tents. ...

Monday morning. This is a beautiful and lovely morning - beautiful emblem of the morning of eternity in heaven. I greatly enjoy it after our cold, chilly weather, which has made me feel doubtful of my capacity, humanly speaking, to endure the campaign, should we remain long in tents. But God, *our God*, does, and will do, all things well; and if it is His pleasure that I remain in the field, He will give me the ability to endure all its fatigues. I hope my little sunshiny face is as bright as this lovely day. Yesterday I heard a good sermon from the chaplain of the Second Regiment, and at night I went over to Colonel Garland's regiment of Longstreet's Brigade, and heard an excellent sermon from the Rev. Mr. Granberry,[10] of the Methodist church, of whom you may have heard me speak in times past. ...

26th. I did not have room enough in my last letter, nor have I time this morning, to write as much as I desired about Dr. Dabney's[11] sermon yesterday. His text was from Acts, seventh chapter and fifth verse. He stated that the word God being in italics indicated that it was not in the original, and he thought it would have been better not to have been in the translation. It would have read: 'Calling upon and saying, Lord Jesus, receive my spirit.' He spoke of Stephen, the first martyr under the new dispensation, like Abel, the first under the old, dying by the hand of violence, and then drew a graphic picture of his probably broken limbs, mangled flesh and features, conspiring to heighten his agonizing sufferings. But in the midst of this intense pain, God, in His infinite wisdom and mercy, permitted him to see the heavens opened, so that he might behold the glory of God, and Jesus, of whom he was speaking, standing on the right hand of God. Was not such a heavenly vision enough to make him forgetful of his sufferings? He beautifully and forcibly described the death of the righteous, and as forcibly that of the wicked. ...

Strangers as well as Lexington friends are very kind to me. I think about eight days since a gentleman sent me a half-barrel of tomatoes, bread, etc., and I received a letter, I am inclined to think from the same, desiring directions how to send a second supply. I received from Colonel Ruff a box of beautifully packed and delicately flavored plums;

---

10   Rev. J.C. Granberry was a chaplain in the Army of Northern Virginia. He was wounded in the war and taken prisoner.

11   Robert Lewis Dabney (1820-1898) was a Presbyterian theologian and professor of church history at Union Seminary, then located in Virginia. During the Civil War he served as a chaplain in the Confederate Army and, in 1862, as Jackson's chief of staff.

also a bottle of blackberry vinegar from the Misses B____.
What I need is a more grateful heart to the 'Giver of every
good and perfect gift.'[12]

October 14th. I am going to write a letter to the very sweetest
little woman I know, the only sweetheart I have; can you guess
who she is? I tell you, I would like to see my sunshine, even
this brightest of days. My finger has been healed over for
some time, and I am blest by an ever-kind Providence with the
use of it, though it is still partially stiff. I hope, however, in the
course of time, that I shall be again blest with its perfect use.
... If I get into winter-quarters, will little ex-Anna Morrison
come and keep house for me, and stay with me till the opening
of the campaign of 1862? Now, remember, I don't want to
change housekeepers. I want the same one all the time. I am
very thankful to that God who withholds no good thing from
me (though I am so utterly unworthy and ungrateful) for
making me a major-general in the Provisional Army of the
Confederate States. The commission dates from the 7th of
October. ...

November 4th. This morning I received orders to proceed to
Winchester. I am assigned to the command of the military
district of the Northern frontier, between the Blue Ridge
and the Allegheny Mountains, and I hope to have my little
dove with me this winter. How do you like the programme?
I trust I may be able to send for you after I get settled.
I don't expect much sleep to-night, as my desire is to
travel all night, if necessary, for the purpose of reaching
Winchester before day to-morrow. My trust is in God for
the defense of that country [the Shenandoah Valley]. I shall
have great labor to perform, but, through the blessing of our
ever-kind Heavenly Father, I trust that He will enable me to
accomplish it.

---

12   James 1:17.

November 9th. ... I trust that my darling little wife feels more gratitude to our kind Heavenly Father than pride or elation at my promotion. Continue to pray for me, that I may live to glorify God more and more, by serving Him and our country. ... If you were only here, you would have a very nice house. ... And if your husband stays here this winter, he hopes to send one of his aides for one little somebody. You know very well who I mean by 'little somebody.'

And now for an answer to your questions; and without stating your questions, I will answer them. My command is enlarged, and embraces the Valley District, and the troops of this district constitute the Army of the Valley; but my command is not altogether independent, as it is embraced in the Department of Northern Virginia, of which General Johnston has command. There are three armies in this department - one under General Beauregard, another under General Holmes, and the third under my command. My headquarters are for the present at Winchester....

During this winter, Anna came to stay with Jackson at Winchester for over two months. The Jacksons stayed with Dr James Graham, a Presbyterian clergyman. In March, Anna returned to Cottage Home.

April 7th. My precious pet, your sickness gives me great concern; but so live that it, and all your trials, may be sanctified to you, remembering that 'our light afflictions, which are but for a moment, work out for us a far more exceeding and eternal weight of glory.'[13] I trust you and all I have in the hands of a kind Providence, knowing that all things work together for the good of His people.

Yesterday was a lovely Sabbath day. Although I had not the privilege of hearing the word of life, yet it felt like a holy Sabbath day, beautiful, serene, and lovely. All it wanted

---

13 2 Corinthians. 4:17.

was the church-bell and God's services in the sanctuary to make it complete. ... Our gallant little army is increasing in numbers, and my prayer is that it may be an army of the living God as well as of its country.

For three months during the spring of 1862, Jackson fought his famous 'Valley Campaign' in the Shenandoah Valley of Virginia. Facing Federal forces three times as large as his, by brilliant strategy Jackson's Confederates outmaneuvered and defeated the Union troops. Jackson wrote Anna descriptions of his military operations while also writing of his love for her and his spiritual concerns.

NEW HARRISONBURG, MAY 19TH

... How I do desire to see our country free and at peace! It appears to me that I would appreciate home more than I have ever done before. Here I am sitting in the open air, writing on my knee for want of a table. ... Yesterday Dr. Dabney preached an excellent sermon from the text: 'Come unto me, all ye that labor and are heavy laden, and I will give you rest.'[14] It is a great privilege to have him with me.

NEAR PORT REPUBLIC, JUNE 10TH

On Sunday, the 8th, an attack was made upon us by a part of Shield's command about seven o'clock A.M., which a kind Providence enabled us to repulse. During the same morning Fremont attacked us from the opposite side, and after several hours' fighting he also was repulsed. Yesterday morning I attacked that part of Shield's force which was near Port Republic, and, after a hotly contested field from near six to ten and a half A.M., completely routed the enemy, who lost eight pieces of artillery during the two days. God has been our shield, and to His name be all the glory. I sent you a telegram yesterday. How I do wish for peace, but only upon the condition of our national independence!

---

14   Matthew 11:28.

Near Weyer's Cave, June 14ᵀᴴ

When I look at the locality of the cave, I take additional interest in it from the fact that my *esposita* was there once. ... Our God has again thrown his shield over me in the various apparent dangers to which I have been exposed. This evening we have religious services in the army for the purpose of rendering thanks to the Most High for the victories with which He has crowned our arms, and to offer earnest prayer that He will continue to give us success, until through His divine blessing, our independence shall be established. Wouldn't you like to get home again?

After their success in the Shenandoah Valley, Jackson and his men joined General Robert E. Lee's Army of Northern Virginia in the Defense of Richmond. After the Battle of the Seven Days, Union General McClellan withdrew from his attack on the Confederate capital.

Near White Oak Swamp Bridge, June 30ᵀᴴ

An ever-kind Providence has greatly blessed our efforts and given us great reason for thankfulness in having defended Richmond. To-day the enemy is retreating down the Chickahominy towards the James River. Many prisoners are falling into our hands. General D.H. Hill[15] and I are together. I had a wet bed last night, as the rain fell in torrents. I got up about midnight, and haven't seen much rest since. I do trust that our God will soon bless us with an honorable peace, and permit us to be together at home again in the enjoyment of domestic happiness.

You must give fifty dollars for church purposes, and more should you be disposed. Keep an account of the amount, as we must give at least one tenth of our income. I would like very

---

15   D.H. Hill and Jackson had been friends at Lexington, where Hill had been a professor of mathematics at Washington College. Hill's wife, Isabella, was Anna's older sister. Anna had been visiting the Hills when she and Jackson first met in Lexington.

much to see my darling, but hope that God will enable me to remain at the post of duty until, in His own good time, He blesses us with independence. ...

GORDONSVILLE, JULY 28TH

My darling wife, I am just overburdened with work, and I hope you will not think hard at receiving only very short letters from your loving husband. A number of officers are with me, but people keep coming to my tent - though let me say no more. A Christian should never complain. The apostle Paul said, 'I glory in tribulations!'[16] What a bright example for others!

On last Saturday our God again crowned our arms with victory about six miles from Culpepper Court-House. I can hardly think of the fall of Brigadier-General C.S. Winder without tearful eyes. Let us all unite more earnestly in imploring God's aid in fighting our battles for us. The thought that there are so many of God's people praying for His blessing upon the army greatly strengthens and encourages me. The Lord has answered their prayers, and my trust is in Him, that He will continue to do so. If God be for us, who can be against us? That He will still be with us and give us victory until our independence shall be established, and that He will make our nation that people whose God is the Lord, is my earnest and oft-repeated prayer. While we attach so much importance to being free from temporal bondage, we must attach far more to being free from the bondage of sin.

After the second Confederate victory at Manassas or Bull Run, the South took the offensive and entered Maryland. After the bloody battle of Antietam or Sharpsburg, they retreated again to Virginia.

---

16   Romans 5:3.

BUNKER HILL, OCTOBER 13ᵀᴴ

I am sitting in my tent, about twelve miles from our 'war-home,' where you and I spent such a happy winter. The weather is damp, and for the past two days has been rainy and chilly. Yesterday was communion at Mr. Graham's[17] church, and he invited me to be present, but I was prevented from enjoying that privilege. However, I heard an excellent sermon from the Rev. Dr. Stiles. His text was 1st Timothy, chap. ii., 5th and 6th verses. It was a powerful exposition of the Word of God; and when he came to the word '*himself*' he placed an emphasis upon it, and gave it a force which I had never felt before, and I realized that, truly, the sinner who does not, under the Gospel privileges, turn to God deserves the agonies of perdition. The doctor several times, in appealing to the sinner, repeated the 6th verse - 'Who gave *himself* a ransom for all, to be testified in due time.' What more could God do than to give *himself* a ransom? Dr. Stiles is a great revivalist, and is laboring in a work of grace in General Ewell's division. It is a glorious thing to be a minister of the Gospel of the Prince of Peace. There is no equal position in this world.

Colonel Blanton Duncan, of Kentucky, has presented me with two fine field or marine glasses. He has apparently taken a special interest in me.

October 20ᵗʰ. ....Don't trouble yourself about representations that are made of your husband. These things are earthly and transitory. There are real and glorious blessings, I trust, in reserve for us beyond this life. It is best for us to keep our eyes fixed upon the throne of God and the realities of a more glorious existence beyond the verge of time. It is gratifying to be beloved and to have our conduct approved by our

---

17 Pastor of Presbyterian church in Winchester with whom the Jacksons had stayed the previous winter.

fellow-men, but this is not worthy to be compared with the glory that is in reservation for us in the presence of our glorified Redeemer. Let us endeavor to adorn the doctrine of Christ our Savior in all things, knowing that there awaits us 'a far more exceeding and eternal weight of glory.'[18] I would not relinquish the slightest diminution of that glory for all this world can give. My prayer is that such may ever be the feeling of my heart. It appears to me that it would be better for you not to have anything written about me. Let us follow the teaching of inspiration - 'Let another praise thee, and not thine own mouth: a stranger, and not thine own lips.'[19] I appreciate the loving interest that prompted such a desire in my precious darling. ... You have not forgotten my little intimation that we might meet before the end of the year, but I am afraid now that your *esposo* will not be able to leave his command. However, all this is in the hands of the Most High, and my prayer is that He will direct all for His own glory. Should I be prevented from going to see my precious little wife, and mother should grow worse, I wish you to remain with her. In addition to the comfort it would give her, it would also gratify me to know that she was comforted by your being with her. She has my prayers that it may please our Heavenly Father to restore her again to perfect health. Do not send me any more handkerchiefs, socks, or gloves, as I trust I have enough to last until peace. You think you can remember the names of all the ladies who make presents to me, but you haven't heard near all of them. An old lady in Tennessee, of about eighty years, sent me a pair of socks. A few days since a friend in Winchester presented me with a beautiful bridle and martingale for a general officer, according to the Army Regulations. Mr. Porter, of Jefferson, sent me a roll of gray cloth for a suit of

---

18 2 Corinthians. 4:17.

19 Proverbs 27:2.

clothes, and friends are continually sending these things to contribute to my comfort. I mention all this merely to show you how much kindness has been shown me, and to give you renewed cause for gratitude. If I only had you with me in my evenings, it would be such a comfort! I hope it may be my privilege to be in Winchester this winter. The people are so kind, and take a great interest in my *esposita*, and that gratifies me. ... I am in a Sibley tent, which is of a beautiful conical shape, and I am sure you would enjoy being in it for a while.

November 20th. Don't you wish you were here in Winchester? Our headquarters are about one hundred yards from Mr. Graham's, in a large white house back of his, and in full view of our last winter's quarters, where my *esposa* used to come up and talk with me. Wouldn't it be nice for you to be here again? but I don't know how long you could remain. ... I hope to have the privilege of joining in prayer for peace at the time you name, and trust that all our Christian people will; but peace should not be the chief object of prayer in our country. It should aim more especially to implore God's forgiveness of our sins, and make our people a holy people. If we are but His, all things work together for the good of our country, and no good thing will He withhold from it.

On November 23, 1862, Anna gave birth to a daughter whom she named Julia, after Jackson's mother.

December 4th. ... Oh! how thankful I am to our kind Heavenly Father for having spared my precious wife and given us a little daughter! I cannot tell you how gratified I am, nor how much I wish I could be with you and see my two darlings. But while this pleasure is denied me, I am thankful it is accorded to you to have the little pet, and I hope it may be a great deal of company and comfort to its mother. Now don't exert yourself to write to me, for to know that you were taxing yourself to write would give me more pain than the letter would pleasure, *so you must not do it.* But you must *love your esposo* in the meantime. ... I expect you are just made up now with that baby. Don't you wish your husband wouldn't claim any part of it, but let you have the sole ownership? Don't you regard it as the most precious little creature in the world? Do not spoil it, and don't let anybody tease it. Don't permit it to have a bad temper. How I would love to see the darling little thing! Give her many kisses for her father.

At present I am about fifty miles from Richmond, and one mile from Guiney's Station, on the railroad from Richmond to Fredericksburg. Should I remain here, I do hope you and baby can come to see me before spring, as you can come on the railroad. Wherever I go, God gives me kind friends. The people here show me great kindness. I receive invitation after invitation to dine out, and spend the night, and a great many provisions are sent me, including nice cakes, tea, loaf-sugar, etc., and the socks and gloves and handkerchiefs still come!

I am so thankful to our ever-kind Heavenly Father for having so improved my eyes as to enable me to write at night. He continually showers blessings upon me; and that *you* should have been spared, and our darling little daughter given us, fills my heart with overflowing gratitude. If I know my unworthy self, my desire is to live *entirely and unreservedly to God's glory.* Pray, my darling, that I may so live.

December 10th. This morning I received a charming letter from my darling daughter, Julia.[20]... Do not set your affections upon her, except as a gift from God. If she absorbs too much of hearts, God may remove her from us.

On December 13 Jackson fought in the Battle of Fredericksburg, securing a great Confederate victory. The battle was on a Saturday, and Jackson did not write Anna the news of the battle until the following Tuesday.

---

20   Anna was staying with her sister in North Carolina. Her sister wrote Jackson in Julia's name until Anna was well enough to resume her correspondence.

December 16th. Yesterday, I regret to say, I did not send you a letter. I was on the front from before dawn until after sunset. The enemy, through God's blessing, was repulsed at all points on Saturday, and I trust that our Heavenly Father will continue to bless us. We have renewed reason for gratitude to Him for my preservation during the last engagement. We have to mourn the deaths of Generals Maxey Gregg and Thomas R.R. Cobb. The enemy has recrossed to the north side of the Rappahannock. ... I was made very happy at hearing through my baby daughter's last letter that she had entirely recovered, and that she 'no longer saw the doctor's gray whiskers.' I was much gratified to learn that she was beginning to notice and smile when caressed. I tell you, I would love to caress her and see her smile. Kiss the little darling for her father and give my grateful love to sister H_____.

Christmas, 1862. Yesterday I received the baby's letter with its beautiful lock of hair. How I do want to see that precious baby! and I do earnestly pray for peace. Oh that our country was such a Christian, God-fearing people as it should be! Then might we very speedily look for peace. Last evening I received a letter from Dr. Dabney, saying: 'One of the highest gratifications both Mrs. Dabney and I could enjoy would be another visit from Mrs. Jackson when her health is re-established,' and he invites me to meet you there. He and Mrs. Dabney are very kind, but it appears to me that it is better for me to remain with my command so long as the war continues, if our gracious Heavenly Father permits. The army suffers immensely by absentees. If all our troops, officers, and men, were at their posts, we might, through God's blessing, expect a more speedy termination of the war. The temporal affairs of some are so deranged as to make a strong plea for their returning home for a short time; but our God has greatly blessed me and mine during my absence;

and whilst it would be a great comfort to see you and our darling daughter, and others in whom I take special interest, yet duty appears to require me to remain with my command. It is important that those at headquarters set an example by remaining at the post of duty.

Dr. Dabney writes: 'Our little prayer-meeting is still meeting daily to pray for our army and leaders.' This prayer-meeting may be the means of accomplishing more than an army. I wish that such existed everywhere. How it does cheer my heart to hear of God's people praying for our cause and for me! I greatly prize the prayers of the pious.

December 29th. Yesterday I had the privilege of attending divine service in a church near General Hill's headquarters, and enjoyed the services very much. Dr. White says in a recent letter that our pew at home has been constantly occupied by Wheeling refugees. I am gratified to hear it. He also adds, 'How we would rejoice to see you and our dear friend, Mrs. Jackson, again in that pew, and in the lecture-room at prayer-meetings! We still meet every Wednesday afternoon to pray for our army, and especially for our general.' May every needful blessing rest upon you and our darling child is the earnest prayer of your devoted husband.

January 6th [1863]. I am very thankful to our kind Heavenly Father for good tidings from you and baby - specially that she is restored again to health, and I trust that we all three may so live as most to glorify His holy name. ... My ears are still troubling me, but I am very thankful that my hearing is as good as usual, and from my appearance one would suppose that I was perfectly well. Indeed, my health is essentially good, but I do not think I shall be able in future to stand what I have already stood, although, with the exception of the increased sensitiveness of my ears, my health has improved. I am sorry to hear that dear mother's health does not improve. ... We have several cases of smallpox at Guiney's, and I expect you will have to give up all idea of coming to see me until spring, as I fear it would be too much of a risk for you and baby to travel up here. ...

January 17th. Yesterday I had the pleasure of receiving a letter from my *esposita* four days after it was written. Doesn't it look as if Confederate mails are better than United States mails? Don't you remember how long it took for letters to come from Charlotte to Lexington under the old *regime*? I derive an additional pleasure in reading a letter from the conviction that it has not traveled on the Sabbath. How delightful will be our heavenly home, where everything is sanctified! ...I am gratified at hearing that you have commenced disciplining the baby. Now be careful, and don't let her conquer *you*. She must not be permitted to have that will of her own, of which you speak. How I would love to see the little darling, whom I love so tenderly, though I have never seen her; and if the war were only over, I tell you, I would hurry down to North Carolina, to see my wife and baby. I have much work to do. Lieutenant-Colonel Faulkner is of great service to me in making out my reports. Since he is my senior adjutant-general, Pendleton is promoted to a majority, and is the junior adjutant-general. ...I regret to see our Winchester friends again in the hands of the enemy. I trust that, in answer to prayer, our country will soon be blessed with peace. If we were only that obedient people that we should be, I would, with increased confidence, look for a speedy termination of hostilities. Let us pray more and live more to the glory of God. ... I am still thinking and thinking about that baby, and do want to see her. Can't you send her to me by express? There is an express line all the way to Guiney's. I am glad to hear that she sleeps well at night, and doesn't disturb her mother. But it would be better not to call her a *cherub*; no earthly being is such. I am also gratified that Hetty is doing well. Remember me to her, and tell her that, as I didn't give her a present last Christmas, I intend giving her two next. ... Don't you accuse my baby of not being *brave*. I do hope she will get over her fear of strangers. If, before strangers take her, you would give them something to please her, and thus make her have pleasant associations with them, and seeing them frequently, I trust she would lose her timidity. It is gratifying that she is growing well, and I am thankful she is so bright and knowing. I do wish I could see her funny ways, and hear her 'squeal out with delight' at seeing the little chickens. I am sometimes afraid that you will make such an idol of that baby that God will take her from us. Are *you* not afraid of it? Kiss her for her father. ...

February 3ᵈ· In answer to the prayers of God's people, I trust He will soon give us peace. I haven't seen my wife for nearly a year - my home in nearly two years, and have never seen our darling little daughter; but it is important that I, and those at headquarters, should set an example of remaining at the post of duty. ... My old Stonewall Brigade has built a log church. As yet I have not been in it. I am much interested in reading Hunter's 'Life of Moses.' It is a delightful book, and I feel more improved in reading it than by an ordinary sermon. I am thankful to say that my Sabbaths are passed more in meditation than formerly. Time thus spent is genuine enjoyment.

February 7ᵗʰ. This has been a beautiful spring day. I have been thinking lately about gardening. If I were at home, it would be time for me to begin to prepare the hot-bed. Don't you remember what interest we used to take in our hot-bed? If we should be privileged to return to our old home, I expect we would find many changes. ... Just to think our baby is nearly three months old. Does she notice and laugh much? You have never told me how much she looks like her mother. I tell you, I want to know how she looks. If you could hear me talking to my *esposa* in the mornings and evenings, it would make you laugh, I'm sure. It is funny the way I talk to her when she is hundreds of miles away. ... I am so much concerned about mother's health as to induce me to recommend a leave of absence for Joseph. I send this note by him, and also send the baby a silk handkerchief. I have thought that as it is brightly colored, it might attract her attention. Remember, it is her first present from her father, and let me know if she notices it.

April 10th. I trust that God is going to bless us with great success, and in such a manner as to show that it is all His gift; and I trust and pray that it will lead our country to acknowledge Him, and to live in accordance with His will as revealed in the Bible. There appears to be an increased religious interest among our troops here. Our chaplains have weekly meetings on Tuesdays; and the one of this week was more charming than the preceding one.

During the winter and spring of 1862-1863, Jackson had time to especially encourage Christian devotion and worship among the soldiers. Not only did he hold regular devotions and prayer meetings for his own staff, but he encouraged evangelical chaplains to actively minister to the men through preaching, prayer, and personal work. A revival swept through the army, and many were converted to Christ.

On April 20, 1863, Anna and baby Julia visited Jackson at the home of William Yerby, south of Fredericksburg. It had been over a year since Anna and Tom had been together, and Jackson was able to see his little daughter Julia for the first time. The little family enjoyed a beautiful nine days together. During that time Julia was baptized by Rev. Lacy, Chaplain of Jackson's II Corps. On April 29, Anna and Julia had to leave, since General Hooker had crossed the Rappahannock and a battle seemed imminent.

Before the mother and daughter reached home, while they were staying at Governor Letcher's in Richmond, news came that Jackson had been wounded - accidentally shot by his own men while returning from reconnoitering the field before the battle of Chancellorsville. Anna and Julia reached Guiney's Station May 7.

Jackson's injured arm had been amputated, and pneumonia began to weaken his lungs. Anna read him Scriptures, sang hymns to him, and brought in little Julia to sit on his bed. In spite of the loving care and prayers of many, Jackson worsened. When Jackson and the other Southern soldiers had marched off to war, Anna felt:

> It was a time of keen anguish and fearful apprehension to us whose loved ones had gone forth in such a perilous and desperate undertaking, but one feeling seemed to pervade every heart, that it was a just and righteous cause; and our hope was in God, who 'could save by many or by few,'[21] and to Him the Christian people of the South looked and prayed. That so many united and fervent prayers should have been offered in vain is one of those mysteries which can never be fathomed by finite minds. The mighty Ruler of the nations saw fit to give victory to the strong arm of power, and He makes no mistakes. But for two years I was buoyed up by hope, which was strengthened by my husband's cheerfulness and courageous trust; and when he became more and more useful in the service of his country, I felt that God had a work for him to accomplish, and my trust and prayers grew more confident that his precious life would be spared throughout the war. It was well that I could not foresee the future. It was in mercy that He who knew the end from the beginning did not lift the veil.[22]

Even after his injury, Jackson felt that the Lord still had a purpose for him in the army and that he would recover. Yet, after Jackson on May 10 said, 'Let us cross over the river and rest under the shade of the trees,' he breathed his last. As he had always wished, he died on the Sabbath. His body was taken to Lexington, where he was buried next to his first wife and daughter.

Anna remained a widow for over half a century, beloved and revered as 'Stonewall' Jackson's wife and as the preserver of the memory of a renowned Christian gentleman and soldier.

---

21 I Samuel 14:6.

22 *Memoirs of 'Stonewall' Jackson*, p. 147.

JOHN WINTHROP
AND
MARGARET WINTHROP

(1587-1649)

(C. 1591-1647)

'I have many reasons to make me love you, whereof I will name two:
First, because you love God, and secondly, because you love me.'
Margaret Winthrop

John Winthrop, organizer and first governor of the Puritan Massachusetts Bay Colony, is today most often remembered as the leader who challenged the Puritan colonists to become a 'city on the hill,' a model to the world of Christian charity. He was a businessman and man of affairs in his day, but he had a heart for God. In his work, as in all of life, he sought to live in a God-honoring way. He found that even marriage was to be a means of spiritual improvement.

John was the only son of Anne and Adam Winthrop of Groton Manor, Suffolk, England. The family was involved in the textile and cloth-making industry, and the Winthrop home was always a hospitable place for visiting judges, lawyers, and ministers.[1]

---

1   Winthrop's parents had a very loving relationship. A letter from Anne, his mother, to Adam, his father, shows their deep affection:

I have received, (right dear and well-beloved) from you this week a letter, though short, yet very sweet, which gave me a lively taste of those sweet & comfortable words, which always when you are present with me, or absent from me, you are ever one towards me, & your heart remains always with me. Wherefore laying up this persuasion of

When John was eighteen, his parents arranged his marriage to Mary Forth, daughter and heir of John Forth, Esq. of Great Stambridge. The young couple lived in Essex. Mr Culverwell, the minister there, faithfully taught the Scripture, and under his ministry John developed an insatiable thirst for the Word of God. In 1615, however, after eleven years of marriage and bearing six children (four of whom survived), Mary died and was buried at Groton. John was not yet 28, and his oldest son was not yet nine.

On December 6, 1615, John married Thomasine Clopton; a short year later Thomasine and her infant child died. John was most despondent, but in his lowliness and weakness of spirit he came to better know the strength and grace of Christ.[2] Thomasine's spiritual nature had enriched Winthrop's life, brief though their marriage had been.

The more John Winthrop thought about the love he had known in his two marriages, the more he came to appreciate the love of Christ for him. In Jeremiah 2:2, God seemed to be speaking to him,

---

you in my breast, I will most assuredly, the Lord assisting me by his grace, bear always the like loving heart unto you again, until such time as I may more fully enjoy your loving presence. But in the mean time I will remain as one having a great inheritance, or rich treasure, and it being by force kept from him, or he being in a strange Country, and cannot enjoy it (Robert C. Winthrop, *Life and Letters of John Winthrop*, New York: De Capo Press, 1971, reprint of 1864-1867 edition published by Ticknor and Fields of Boston, Vol. 1, 49; spelling and grammar of the Winthrop quotes have been modernized. For ease in following the chronology of the letters, the place and date of each letter has been placed at the beginning, whereas Winthrop placed them at the end with his signature. The form of the dates has been standardized).

2   Winthrop wrote of this time:

...[God] placed a great affliction upon me, by which he lowered me in my own eyes more than at any time before. He showed me the emptiness of all my gifts and skills; left me neither power nor will, so I became as a weaned child. I could now no more look at what I had been or what I had done, nor be discontented for lack of strength or assurance. Mine eyes were only upon his free mercy in Jesus Christ. I knew I was worthy of nothing; for I knew I could do nothing for him or for myself. I could only mourn and weep to think of free mercy to such a vile wretch as I was...the good Spirit of the Lord breathed upon my soul, and said I should live. Then every promise I thought upon held forth Christ unto me; saying, 'I am thy salvation.' Now my soul could close with Christ, and rest there with sweet content, nor feared any thing, but was filled with joy unspeakable and glorious, and with a spirit of adoption. Not that I could pray with more fervency or more enlargement of heart than sometimes before; but I could now cry, 'My father,'" with more confidence (*Life and Letters*, Vol. 1, 77).

I remember you,
The kindness of your youth,
The love of your betrothal,
When you went after Me in the wilderness,
In a land not sown.

Winthrop realized that earthly marriage was only a mirror of the deep love Christ has for His own - and Christ was ever living, so there was no fear or pain of parting or separation as there was in earthly love.

During this time Winthrop read the Song of Solomon (or Canticles) as a love story between Christ and his soul. He would use many of the images from the Song of Solomon in courting his third wife, Margaret Tyndal, daughter of Sir John Tyndal of Great Maplested in Essex. Apparently, Margaret's family had some reservations about the match. After all, Winthrop had four young children to care for and did not have much wealth or fame. Margaret and her mother, however, shared Winthrop's religious convictions and withstood the family's materialistic objections. Winthrop commended Margaret for her decision to seek after spiritual rather than worldly treasures. The strength of their love was not earthly wealth, but spiritual oneness in Christ.

A week or two before their wedding, John wrote Margaret a letter full of imagery from the Song of Solomon as well as ordinary horticulture (some at first glance not particularly romantic, but really quite so when considered in their full meaning):

Groton where I wish you. April 4, 1618.
To my most beloved Mrs. Margaret Tyndall at Great Maplested, Essex.
Grace, mercy, and peace, etc.:
My only beloved Spouse, my most sweet friend, and faithful companion of my pilgrimage,... I wish you a most plentiful increase of all true comfort in the love of Christ, with a large and prosperous addition of whatsoever happiness the sweet estate of holy wedlock, in the kindest society of

a loving husband, may afford you. Being filled with the joy of your love, and wanting opportunity of more familiar communion with you, which my heart fervently desires, I am constrained to ease the burden of my mind by this poor help of my scribbling pen. ...

And now, my sweet Love, let me a while solace myself in the remembrance of your love, of which this spring time of acquaintance can put forth as yet no more but the leaves and blossoms, while the fruit lies wrapped up in the tender bud of hope. A little more patience will disclose this good fruit, and bring it to some maturity. Let it be our care and labor to preserve these hopeful buds from the beasts of the field, and from frosts and other injuries of the air, lest our fruit fall off before it is ripe, or lose anything in the beauty and pleasantness of it. Let us pluck up such nettles and thorns as would defraud our plants of their due nourishment. Let us prune off superfluous branches ... the plenty and goodness of our fruit shall recompense us abundantly.

Our trees are planted in a fruitful soil. The ground and pattern of our love, is no other but that between Christ and his dear spouse,[3] of whom she speaks as she finds him, My beloved is mine and I am his. Love was their banqueting house, love was their wine, love was their ensign [Cant. 2]. ... Love was his embracings; love was her refreshings. Love made him see her; love made her seek him [Jer. 2:2; Ezek. 16]. Love made him wed her; love made her follow him. Love made him her savior; love makes her his servant [John 3:16; Deut. 10:12]. Love bred of fellowship, let love continue it, and love shall increase it, until death dissolve it. ...

Christ in his love so fill our hearts with holy hunger and true appetite, to eat and drink with him and of him in this

---

3   Winthrop here is following the image of the Church as the Bride of Christ and following a long Christian tradition of interpreting the Biblical book of *Canticles* or the *Song of Solomon* as not simply a poem of love between a man and woman, but as an allegory of the love between Christ and His Church.

his sweet Love feast, which we are now preparing unto, that when our love feast shall come, Christ himself may come into us, and sup with us and we with him.[4] So shall we be merry indeed. (O my sweet Spouse) can we esteem each other's love, as worthy recompense of our best mutual affections, and can we not discern so much of Christ's exceeding and undeserved love, as may cheerfully allure us to love him above all? ...

Lastly for my farewell (for you see my reluctance to part with you makes me to be tedious) take courage and cheer up your heart in the Lord. You know that Christ your best husband can never fail you. He never dies, so there can be no grief at parting. He never changes, so once beloved and ever the same. His ability is ever infinite, so the dowry and inheritance of his sons and daughters can never be diminished. ...This is one end why I write so much unto you, that if there should be any decay in kindness through my default and slackness hereafter, you might have some patterns of our first love by you, to help the recovery of such diseases. Let our trust be wholly in God, and let us constantly follow him by our prayers, complaining and moaning unto him our own poverty, imperfections and unworthiness, until his fatherly affection breaks forth upon us, and he speaks kindly to the hearts of his poor servant and handmaid, for the full assurance of Grace and peace through Christ Jesus, to whom I now leave you (my sweet Spouse and only beloved). God send us a safe and comfortable meeting on Monday morning. Farewell. Remember my love and duty to my Lady your good mother, with all kind and due salutations to your uncle E. and all your brothers and sisters.

Your husband by promise,[5]
John Winthrop

---

4   Winthrop here alludes to the sacrament of Communion which was part of the marriage ceremony.

5   Robert C. Winthrop, editor of *Life and Letters of John Winthrop*, commenting on his ancestor's courtship letters wrote, '...most striking evidence, certainly, do they bring to that deep-seated and prevailing love of God in his heart, which strengthened and purified all his other affections, and which seemed itself to be purified and strengthened in turn, even by those very earthly ties and domestic attachments which have so often estranged other hearts from the highest objects of their love (Vol. 1, 140).'

John and Margaret were married at Great Maplested and arrived at Groton on April 24, 1618, beginning thirty years of domestic happiness. Margaret bore John four sons, Stephen, Adam, Deane, and Samuel, adding to his three sons and a daughter by his first wife. Shortly after his marriage to Margaret, a depression in the textile industry upset the finances at Groton Manor. Winthrop turned to his legal training to add to the income of his growing family. His professional service brought him often to London, where he also prepared some bills for consideration by Parliament. During his absences, John and Margaret kept up a steady correspondence. There was no mail between Groton and London, so each wrote when there was a messenger available. Though written in the rush of household and professional duties, the letters reflect a deep and abiding Christian love.

> January 23, 1620
>
> To my very loving wife Mrs. Winthrop at Groton in Suffolk.
>
> My truly beloved and dear wife, - I salute you heartily, giving thanks to God who bestowed you upon me, and has continued you unto me, the chiefest of all comforts under the hope of Salvation, which hope cannot be valued. I pray God that these earthly blessings of marriage, health, friendship, etc., may increase our estimation of our better and only ever enduring happiness in heaven, and may quicken up our appetite according to its worth. O my sweet wife, let us rather hearken to the advise of our loving Lord who calls upon us first to seek the kingdom of God, and tells us that one thing is needful. Without it, the gain of the whole world is nothing[6] ... look at the frothy wisdom of this world and the foolishness of such examples as confuse outward prosperity for true happiness. May God keep us from ever swallowing this bait of Satan. Let us look unto the words of God and cleave fast unto it, and so shall we be safe.

---

6   Matthew 6:33; Luke 10:42; Matthew 16:26.

I know you have heard before this of my arrival in London. I thank God we had a prosperous journey and found all well where we came. I doubt not but your desire will be now to hear of my return, which (to deal truly with you) I fear will not be until the middle of next week. The Parliament is put off for a week, and I have many friends to visit in a short time. But my heart is already with you and your little lambs, so I will hasten home with what convenient speed I may. In the mean time, I will not be unmindful of you all, but commend you daily to the blessings and protection of our heavenly Father....

Remember my duty to my father and mother, my love to Mr. Sands[7] and all the rest of my true friends that shall ask of me, and my blessing to our Children. And so giving you commission to conceive more of my Love than I can write, I rest

Your faithful husband,
John Winthrop

As John regularly traveled to London on business, the loving correspondence between husband and wife continued . Only a few of Margaret's letters have survived, though from John's letters it is obvious her correspondence was as faithful as his.

London, October 3, 1623

My Dear Wife,--Your sweet letters (without date) how welcome they were to me I cannot express. Both in regard of the continuance of your health and your little ones, my mother and our whole family, for which I humbly bless and praise our good God and Heavenly father. I do heartily beg of him and trust in him for the continuance of the same mercy to yourself and all the rest. Also in the manifestation of the constancy and increase of your true love wherein (I seriously profess) I do more rejoice than in any earthly blessing. O how I prize the sweet society of so modest and faithful a spouse! O that I could be wise to be thankful and

---

7   Rev. Henry Sands was the pastor at Groton.

improve it, according to that esteem which I have of it when I want it! I am here where I have all outward content, most kind entertainment, good company and good fare, etc. Only the lack of your presence and amiable society makes me weary of all other accomplishments - so dear is your love to me, and so confident am I of the like entertainment my true affections find with you. O that the consideration of these things could make us raise up our spirits to a like conformity of sincerity and fervency in the Love of Christ our Lord and heavenly husband. O that we could delight in him as we do in each other, and that his absence were similarly grievous to us. But the Love of this present world, how it bewitches us and steals away our hearts from him who is our only life and felicity. But I must break off this discourse. The blessed protection and favor of the Lord be still with you and all our family, and bring us together again in peace.... Here is no news but of the Princes being at sea, where [the ship] has been wind bound a great while.[8] So embracing you in true affection of a faithful husband, I will so remain

Yours,
John Winthrop

December 11, 1623

My most Loving and Dear Wife,--I received your kind and welcome letters, and do heartily bless our merciful God for his gracious providence over you and all our family. Oh that we had hearts to love him and trust him as his kindness is towards us. I am sorry that I cannot return to you so soon as I made account, for coming to Childerditch[9] upon Saturday last, I found my Cousin Barfut very ill, & decaying so fast as on Monday morning I could not leave him. So staying with him about noon he comfortably and quietly gave up the Ghost. I saw God's Providence had brought me there to be a stay &

---

8   Prince Charles, the Prince of Wales and heir to the British throne, and the Duke of Buckingham were returning from Spain where they had unsuccessfully attempted to negotiate Charles' marriage to the Spanish Infanta. The proposed marriage of Charles with a daughter of Catholic Spain was very unpopular in England.

9   A parish in Essex County, about twenty miles from London.

comfort to her in that sudden trial, when none of her friends were with her. By this occasion it was Wednesday night before I could get to London, where (I praise God) I found all well except my brother Fones,[10] who is feverish &c, as he used to be. The days are here so short, & the weather so cold, as I can dispatch no business, so that it will be the end of the next week before I can get home. Here is no certain news, but much expected within a few days. Till I come, have care of yourself & little ones (as I know you do). Remember my duty to mother & my love to Mr. Sands & all the rest. So with my kindest Love to my sweet wife, & my blessing to our children, I commend you & all the rest to the blessing & protection of the Lord & rest,

> Your faithful loving husband,
> John Winthrop

Childerditch Jan. I. 1624[11]
To my very loving Wife Mrs. Winthrop at Groton in Suffolk

My sweet Spouse,--I praise our God, and do heartily rejoice in your welfare & of the rest of our family, longing greatly to be with you, whom my soul delights in above all earthly things. These times of separation are harsh and grievous while they last, but they shall make our meeting more comfortable. It will be Monday at night before I can come home. In the mean time my heart shall be with you, as it is always, & as your Love deserves. I am now at Childerditch from whence I cannot go till Saturday. It will be too far to come home, so I intend to keep the Lord's day at Sir Henry Mildmaies .

The news here is of a Parliament to begin the xiith of February next.[12] The Earl of Oxford came out of the Tower

---

10 Thomas Fones was a London apothecary married to John's older sister, Anne.

11 Under the old style calendar in use in Winthrop's day, the new year began in March, not January. Winthrop thus dated this letter 1623. To avoid confusion for the modern reader, the modern practice of dating a year beginning with January has been used throughout.

12 This would be the last Parliament called by King James before his death. It was called to raise money for a war against the Spanish.

upon Tuesday last. Other things I shall relate to you when we meet. Only I thought to write lest you should be troubled at my not coming on Saturday night. Thus commending you and all ours to the gracious blessing & holy providence of our heavenly father, I heartily embrace my sweet wife in the arms of my best affections, ever resting

Your faithful husband,
J Winthrop

Nov. 26. 1624

My sweet Wife,--I bless the Lord for his continued blessings upon you and our family, & thank you for your kind letters. But I know not what to say for myself. I should mend and grow a better husband, having the help & example of so good a wife, but I grow still worse. I was accustomed before, when I was long absent, to make some supply with volumes of Letters, but I can scarcely afford you a few lines. Well, there is no help but by enlarging your patience, & strengthening your good opinion of him, who loves you as his own soul, & should count it his greatest Affliction to live without you. But because you are so dear to him, he must choose rather to leave you for a time, than to enjoy you. I am sorry I must still prolong your expectation, for I cannot come forth of London till Tuesday at soonest. The Lord bless & keep you & all ours & send us a joyful meeting. So I kiss my sweet wife & rest

Your faithful husband,
John Winthrop

...Your Cider was so well liked that we must needs have more as soon as you can.

Winthrop's stays in London increased in 1627, when his brother-in-law Emmanuel Downing helped him secure an appointment as one of three attorneys to the Court of Wards and Liveries, which oversaw estates which had reverted to the King. The Court met four times a year, and each session lasted from three to seven weeks, keeping John often in London.

My dear Husband,--I received your most kind Letter and thank you for it. I wish your work could allow you to come home, but I must wait the time till I may enjoy you, though it cannot be without much want of your beloved presence, which I desire always to have with me. I see it is the will of God that it should be so, which makes me bear it the more patiently, and not any want of love in my beloved Husband. And now my dear I have nothing to write of to you but my love which is already known to you, and it were needless to make relation of that which you are so well assured. I will leave off this discourse for this time. I shall be glad to hear of my daughter Mary,[13] how her match goes forward. We are all here in reasonable good health I praise God, which is the best news I can write you of. I hear that Mr. Appeleton is dead that lived at Sir Robert Crane. He died very suddenly on Saturday being well overnight. And thus with my best love to yourself, brother and sister Downing, my son J[ohn][14] & daughter M[ary], I desire the Lord to continue all your healths and prosper all your affairs and send us a happy meeting. I being sleepy, as you may see by my writing, bid my good Husband good night and commit him to the safe protection of almighty God and rest

your faithful and obedient wife,
Margaret Winthrop

I am doubtful whether to send your horses this week or wait till I hear from you.[15]

---

13   Winthrop's daughter by his first wife, born in 1612.

14   Winthrop's oldest son by his first wife, born in 1606.

15   Margaret would send John's horses to London when he was ready to come home.

To my very loving Husband John Winthrop Esquire at Mr. Downing's house in Fleet Street near the conduit these deliver.

My most kind and loving Husband,--I did receive your most sweet Letter by my brother Gosling, and do praise God for the continuance of your health, and the rest of our friends. I thank the Lord we are also in health, and think long for your coming home. My good husband your love to me does daily give me cause for comfort, and does much increase my love to you, for love lives by love. I were worse than a brute beast if I should not love and be faithful to you, who has deserved so well at my hands. I am ashamed and grieved with myself that I have nothing within or without worthy of you, and yet it pleases you to accept of both and to rest contented. I had need to amend my life and pray to God for more grace that I may not deceive you of those good hopes which you have of me,--a sinful woman, full of infirmities, continually failing of what I desire and what I ought to perform to the Lord and yourself. I hope in God we shall now shortly meet with comfort, for which I shall pray.-- Your horse shall be at London upon Saturday and we shall see you I hope on Tuesday. I will send you up by John that you did write for, and if you think good you may change it for a new one, but do as you think best. If I have anything that may pleasure you at any time you shall willingly have it. If the carrier calls here this week, I will send my sister Downing some puddings to make her some part of amends, because her share was so small in the last. My mother and myself and brother and sister Gosling remember our love to you and all the rest of our friends. My brother Jenney remembers his love to you and would entreat you to deliver this letter here enclosed. And thus with my love and best affections even with a love increasing I take my leave and commit you to the Lord, who is all sufficient and able to preserve you from all danger and send you safe home. Your loving and obedient wife

Margaret Winthrop

I pray remember my blessing and love to my son John.[16]

Most dear and loving Husband,--I cannot express my love to you, as I desire, in these poor, lifeless lines; but I do heartily wish you did see my heart, how true and faithful it is to you, and how much I do desire to be always with you, to enjoy the sweet comfort of your presence, and those helps from you in spiritual and temporal duties, which I am so unfit to perform without you. It makes me to see the want of you, and wish myself with you. But I desire we may be guided by God in all our ways, who is able to direct us for the best; and so I will wait upon him with patience, who is all-sufficient for me. I shall not need to write much to you at this time. My brother Gostling can tell you any thing by word of mouth. I praise God, we are all here in health, as you left us, and are glad to hear the same of you and all the rest of our friends at London. My mother[17] and myself remember our best love to you, and all the rest. Our children remember their duty to you. And thus, desiring to be remembered in your prayers, I bid my husband good night. Little Samuel[18] thinks it is time for me to go to bed; and so I beseech the Lord to keep you in safety, and us all here. Farewell, my sweet husband.

Your obedient wife,
Margaret Winthrop

---

16   After Winthrop's eldest son John attended Trinity College, Dublin; he stayed with his father in London and studied law.

17   This would be Winthrop's mother, since Margaret's mother died in 1620. Throughout, Margaret and John claimed each other's relatives as their own, whether they be brother, sister, children, or parents.

18   Samuel was baptized Aug. 26, 1627.

Groton, November 22

My most sweet Husband,--How dearly welcome your kind letter was to me, I am not able to express. The sweetness of it did much refresh me. What can be more pleasing to a wife, than to hear of the welfare of her best beloved, and how he is pleased with her poor endeavors! I blush to hear myself commended, knowing my own wants. But it is your love that conceives the best, and makes all things seem better than they are. I wish that I may be always pleasing to you, and that those comforts we have in each other may be daily increased, as far as they be pleasing to God. I will use that speech to you that Abigail did to David, I will be a servant to wash the feet of my lord.[19] I will do any service wherein I may please my good husband. I confess I cannot do enough for you, but you are pleased to accept the will for the deed, and rest contented.

I have many reasons to make me love you, whereof I will name two: First, because you love God, and secondly, because you love me. If these two were wanting, all the rest would be eclipsed. But I must leave this discourse and go about my household affairs. I am a bad housewife to be so long from them, but I must needs borrow a little time to talk with you, my sweet heart. The term is more than half done. I hope your business draws to an end. It will be but two or three weeks before I see you, though they be long ones. God will bring us together in his good time, for which time I shall pray. I thank the Lord, we are all in health. We are very glad to hear so good news of our son Henry.[20] The Lord make us thankful for all his mercies to us and ours. And thus, with my mother's and my own best love to yourself and all the rest, I shall leave scribbling. The weather being cold, makes me make haste. Farewell, my good husband. The Lord keep you.

Your obedient wife, Margaret Winthrop

---

19 I Samuel 25.

20 Henry, who was born in 1607 and was Winthrop's second son, had gone to Barbados to try and make a fortune in tobacco.

I have not received the box; but I will send for it. I send up a turkey and some cheese. I pray send my son Forth[21] such a knife as mine is....

The friction between King Charles and Parliament intensified in 1628. Charles' acceptance of the Petition of Right seemed a Parliamentary victory, but Charles was determined to assert what he considered his royal prerogative.

To my dear and very loving Husband John Winthrop Esquire at Mr. Downings[22] house in Fleet Street right over against the Conduit these deliver--London

My beloved and good Husband, ... I do join with you in beseeching the Lord to direct our ways and thoughts aright herein, and that we may submit unto his holy will in this and all other things, to do that may be for his glory and the comfort of ourselves and others. I do see yours and the rest of my friends' great love and care of me and of all ours, in that you are so mindful of our good, which does more and more knot my affections to you. I pray God I may walk so as I may be worthy of all your loves.... Upon the best consideration I can take, I have resolved to stay here all winter, in regard that my little one is very young[23] and the ways very bad to remove such things as we shall stand in need of, and we shall leave things very unsettled, and to keep two families will be very chargeable to us. And so I think it will be our best course to remove in the spring, and in the mean time commend it to God....

I have received your kind letter by my brother Gosling for which I heartily thank you and for my good sermon which you sent with it. You do daily manifest your love to me and care

---

21 Forth, who was born in 1609 and was Winthrop's third son, was in college at Cambridge, studying to be a minister.

22 There was no apostrophe in the original. The name is 'Downing', so it would be appropriate today to have the name read 'Mr. Downing's house'.

23 Samuel was barely a year old.

for my spiritual good, as well as temporal. ... I desire of God I may choose the better part which cannot be taken from me, which will stand me in stead when all other things fail for me. ... I cannot but with grief bear your long absence, but I hope that this will be the last time we shall be so long asunder, which does somewhat stay and comfort me. The Lord grant I may find sweetness in Christ Jesus my spiritual Husband, who is always with me and never fails me in time of need, nor will fail me unto the end of my life or the life to come. My good mother commends her love to you all and thanks you for her tobacco. She would pray you to be careful of yourself that you take no cold. I desire to have my love very kindly remembered to my brother Downing and sister, my brother Fones and sister, and all my cousins. I praise God we continue still in health. I think very long to hear of our sons at sea.[24] I pray God send us good news of them. And thus with my best affection remembered to my dear Husband I take my leave and commit you to God.

Your faithful and obedient wife,

Margaret Winthrop.

May 1, 1628

Loving and most dear Husband,--Now in this solitary and uncomfortable time of your long absence, I have no other means to show my love but in these poor fruits of my pen, with which I am not able to express my love as I desire, but I shall endeavor always to make my duty known to you in some measure though not answerable to your deserts and love. Although it pleases God to part us for a time, I hope he will bring us together again and so provide that we may not be often asunder, if it may be for our good and his glory. I long to hear of you and of your safe coming to London.

---

24   John had wanted to go with John Endecott and other Puritans sent by the New England Company to New England, but when his father urged him not to settle permanently in New England, he took a tour of the Mediterranean.

I will not look for any long letters this term because I pity your poor hand. If I had it here I would make more of it than ever I did, and bind it up very softly for fear of hurting it….I thank God we are all here in health, only little Sam, who has been very sick, but I hope he will do well again. I am glad I did not wean him for he will now take nothing but the breast. Thus it pleases the Lord to exercise us with one affliction after another in love; lest we should forget ourselves and love this world too much, and not set our affections on heaven where all true happiness is for ever. ... with my mothers and my own best love to you and the rest of our friends, I commit you to the Lord and rest.

Your Obedient Wife,
Margaret Winthrop

To my very loving Husband John Winthrop Esq. at Mr. Downings.

My most dear and loving Husband,--I do bless and praise God for the continuance of your health, and for the safe delivery of my good sister Downing. It was very welcome news to us. I thank the Lord we are all here reasonably well. My poor Stephen is up today.[25] Amy[26] has had a very bad fever but is well again. I hope the Lord will hear our prayers and be pleased to stay his hand in this visitation, which if he please to do we shall have great cause of thankfulness. But I desire in this and all other things to submit unto his holy will. It is the Lord, let him do what seems good in his own eyes. He will do nothing but that shall be for our good if we had hearts to trust in him, & all shall be for the best whatsoever it shall please him to exercise us withal. He wounds & he can heal. He has never failed to do us good, and now he will not shake us off, but continue the same God still that he has been heretofore.

---

25 Margaret and John's first son together, born in 1619. Stephen apparently had been ill and was now better.

26 Margaret's maid servant.

The Lord sanctify unto us whatsoever it shall please him to send unto us, that we may be the better for it & furthered in our course to heaven.

I am sorry for the hard condition of Rochelle.[27] The Lord help them & fight for them & then none shall prevail against them or overcome them. In vain they fight that fight against the Lord, who is a mighty God and will destroy all his enemies. And now my dear husband I have nothing but my dearest affections to send you--with many thanks for your kind letters, praying you to accept a little for a great deal. My will is good but I lack the ability to show and express it to you as I desire. I pray remember me to my brothers & sisters, & tell my brother Fones I thank him for the things he send [sic], & so I bid my good husband farewell & commit him to God.

Your loving and obedient wife,
Margaret Winthrop

I send up a turkey & 2 capons & a cheese. The carrier is paid.

April 28, 1629

My good Wife,--Although I wrote to you last week by the carrier of Hadleigh, yet, having so fit opportunity, I must needs write to you again, for I do esteem one little, sweet, short letter of yours (such as the last was) to be well worthy [sic] two or three from me. How it is with us, these bearers[28] can inform you, so I may write the less. They were married on Saturday last, and intend to stay with you till towards the end of the term, for it will be yet six weeks before they can take their voyage. Labor to keep my son at home as much as you can, especially from Hadleigh. ...

---

27   The Huguenot citadel of LaRochelle in France, where English ships joined the French in their fight. Richelieu took LaRochelle in 1628, and the Huguenots were in dire straits. Huguenots were French Protestants for whom the Puritans had great sympathy.

28   Henry and his new wife, Elizabeth Fones. Henry's adventure in Barbados had not been successful, and he returned to London to indulge in riotous living. Pretending his cousin Elizabeth was pregnant, Henry hurriedly married her. Winthrop cut off Henry's support but did allow the couple to live at Groton.

It grieves me that I have not liberty to make better expression of my love to you, who are more dear to me than all earthly things. But I will endeavor that my prayers may supply the defect of my pen, which will be of best use to us both, inasmuch as the favor and blessing of our God is better than all things besides. My trust is in his mercy, that, upon the faith of his gracious promise, and the experience of his fatherly goodness, he will be our God to the end, to carry us along through this course of our pilgrimage, in the peace of a good conscience, and that, in the end of our race, we shall safely arrive at the haven of eternal happiness. We see how frail and vain all earthly good things are. There is no means to avoid the loss of them in death, nor the bitterness which accompanies them in the cares and troubles of this life. Only the fruition of Jesus Christ and the hope of heaven can give us true comfort and rest. The Lord teach us wisdom to prepare for our change, and to lay up our treasure there, where our abiding must be forever. I know you expect troubles here, and, when one affliction is over, to meet with another. But remember what our Savior tells us, 'Be of good comfort, I have overcome the world.'[29] See his goodness. He has conquered our enemies beforehand, and by faith in him, we shall assuredly prevail over them all. Therefore (my sweet wife), raise up your heart, and be not dismayed at the crosses you meet within family affairs or otherwise.[30] But still fly to him, who will take up your burden for you. Go on cheerfully, in obedience to his holy will, in the course he has set you. Peace shall come. You shall rest as in your bed. In the mean time, he will not fail

---

29   John 16:33.

30   The Winthrops had just undergone a series of family losses. Winthrop's brother-in-law Thomas Fones died in London April 15, 1629. Winthrop's mother died at Groton April 19. On the 25th, Henry married Elizabeth (Thomas Fones' daughter) to take her to his plantation in the West Indies.

nor forsake you.[31] But my time is past. I must leave you. So I commend you and all yours to the gracious protection and blessing of the Lord. All our friends here salute you. Salute you ours from me. Farewell, my good wife. I kiss and love you with the kindest affection, and rest

Your faithful husband,
John Winthrop

May 15, 1629

My dear Wife, I am truly persuaded, God will bring some heavy Affliction upon this land, & that speedily. Be of good comfort, the hardest that can come shall be a means to mortify this body of corruption, which is a thousand times more dangerous to us than any outward tribulation, & to brng us into nearer communion with our Lord Jesus Christ, & more assurance of his kingdom. If the Lord sees it will be good for us, he will provide a shelter & a hiding place for us & others, as a Zoar for Lott, Sarephtah for his prophet, &c.[32] If not, yet he will not forsake us. Though he correct us with the rods of men, yet if he take not his mercy and lovingkindness from us we shall be safe. He only is all sufficient. If we have him we have all things. If he sees it not good to cut our portion, in these things below, equal to the largeness of our desires, yet if he please to frame our minds to the portion he allots us, it will be as well for us.

I thank you for your kind letter. I am going to Westminster, & must here break off. I would have my son H[enry] to be here on Tuesday that I may go out of town on Wednesday or Thursday next. If Mary her gown be made I will send it

---

31 Hebrews 13:5.

32 Genesis 19:30; I Kings 17. In March, 1629, a week before King Charles dissolved Parliament, he granted a royal charter for a group of Puritans to form the Massachusetts Bay Company in New England. At a time when the Tower was loaded with Puritan prisoners, the granting of the Massachusetts Bay Charter seemed an unmistakable work of Providence. When he arrived in London, Winthrop undoubtedly became involved in discussions with those planning to establish a Puritan settlement in America.

down by Smith this week, or else next, with other things.... in very much haste, I end and commend you & all ours to the gracious protection & blessing of the Lord--so I kiss my sweet wife, & think long till I see you--farewell.

Yours,

John Winthrop

I thank you for our Turkey.

June 5, 1629

To my very loving wife Mrs. Winthrop at Groton in Suffolk

You may marvel that you had no Letter from me by my Son [Henry], but I know you will not impute it to any decay of love, or neglect of you, who are more precious to me than any other thing in this world. But the uncertainty of his journey, & the dislike of his ill course, made me strange myself towards him. I praise God I came here safely, & am in good health as all our friends here are (who desire to be kindly remembered to you). I hope my son has put away his man, for he promised he would, & that he would amend his life. I beseech the Lord to give him grace so to do, otherwise he will soon be undone. I am still more confirmed in that course which I propounded to you [emigration to America], & so are my brother and sister D[owning]. The good Lord direct and bless us in it.

I received a letter from Forth's Tutor, in which he complains of his longer absence, which he finds does him much hurt both in his learning & manners, & wishes me to send him speedily, for he says he has provided him a chamber in the College. I pray you speak with him, & do as may be fittest, for if he intends not the ministry, I have no great mind to send him any more. If he does, let him go so soon as he can. I have now received your sweet letter, which I heartily thank you for, & do with all thankfulness acknowledge the goodness of the

Lord towards us in his blessing upon you & all ours, which I shall labor the continuance of to the best of my power, & so far as my poor prayers can give furtherance. I am sorry I cannot write to you as I desire, but you will bear with me the rather that I think my Office is gone, so I shall not wrong you so much with my absence as I have done. I will send you some pepper in my son's box, & so with my blessing to my sons and daughters, salutations to all our good friends, & my most entire Affections to yourself, I commend you to the grace and blessing of the Lord & rest

Your faithful husband,
John Winthrop

To his very loving Wife, Mrs. Winthrop, at her House in Groton.

My good Wife... Blessed be the Lord, our good God, who watches over us in all our ways to do us good, and to comfort us with his manifold blessings, not taking occasion by our sins to punish us as we deserve. Through his mercy it is, that I continue in health, and that, to my great joy, I hear well of you and our family. The Lord teach us the right use of all his blessings, and so temper our affections towards the good things of this life, as our greatest joy may be, that our names are in the book of life, that we have the good will of our heavenly Father, that Christ Jesus is ours, and that by him we have right to all things. Then, come what will, we may have joy and confidence.

My sweet wife, I am sorry that I cannot now appoint the time, that I hope to return, which cannot be the next week, though it is likely that my sister Fones, or some of her company, will come down then. But you shall hear more the beginning of next week.

For news I have but one to write of, but that will be more welcome to you than a great deal of other. My office is gone, and my chamber, and I shall be a saver in them both.[33] So, as I hope, we shall now enjoy each other again, as we desire. The Lord teach us to improve our time and society to more use for our mutual comfort, and the good of our family, etc., than before. It is now bed time, but I must lie alone, therefore I make less haste. Yet I must kiss my sweet wife. And so, with my blessing to our children, and salutation to all our friends, I commend you to the grace and blessing of the Lord, and rest,

Your faithful husband,
Jo. Winthrop.

June 22, 1629

My good Wife,--Blessed be the Lord our God for his great mercy still continued to us and ours. O that we could consider aright of his kindness, that we might know our happiness in being the children of such a father, & so tenderly beloved of the All sufficient, but we must needs complain. Oh this flesh, this frail, sinful flesh, that obscures the beauty & brightness of so great glory & goodness! I thank you for your most kind & sweet Letter, the stamp of that amiable affection of a most loving wife. I assure you, your labor of love (tho' it be very great) shall not be lost, so far as the prayers & endeavors of a faithful husband can tend to requital. But I must limit the length of my desires to the shortness of my leisure, otherwise I should not know when to end. I trust, in the Lord, the time of our wished meeting will be shortly, but my occasions are such as you must have patience till the end of next week, though I shall strive to shorten it, if possible I may. After that, I hope, we shall never part so long again, till we part for a better meeting in

---

33   In June, 1629, Winthrop lost his office as an Attorney to the Court of Wards. Possibly he lost his position because of the Puritans' and Parliament's growing opposition to King Charles' government; possibly he resigned. Winthrop's letters clearly show he sees a crisis coming in England, and he expects to be in the thick of the events.

heaven. But where we shall spend the rest of our short time I know not. The Lord, I trust, will direct us in mercy. My comfort is that you are willing to be my companion in what place or condition soever, in weal or in woe. Be it what it may, if God be with us, we need not fear. His favor, & the kingdom of heaven will be alike & happiness enough to us & ours in all places. ... [Henry] is in London, but I have seen him but twice. I know not what he does or what he intends. I mourn for his sins & the misery that he will soon bring upon himself & his wife. Our friends here are all in health (God be praised) & desire to be commended to you, so with my love & blessing to our children, salutation to all our friends, my brother and sister Gosling &c, I commend you to the good Lord and kiss my sweet wife & rest

Your faithful husband,

Jo. Winthrop

After leaving the Court of Wards and Liveries, Winthrop and Emmanuel Downing spent two weeks in Lincolnshire with other Puritans evaluating large-scale emigration to New England. Winthrop spent the summer and fall writing his 'Arguments for the Plantation of New England,' which set forth the reasons for Puritan emigration.

October [1629]

My dear Wife,--I praise the Lord that I hear of your welfare, and of the rest of our family. I thank you for your most kind letter. I am sorry I cannot come down to you, as I hoped, but there is no remedy. The Lord so disposes as I must stay yet (I doubt) a fortnight, but, assure yourself, not one day more than I must needs.

I pray you have patience. God, in his due time, will bring us together in peace. We are now agreed with the merchants, and stay only to settle our affairs. I have not one quarter of an hour's time to write to you. Therefore you must bear with me, and supply all defects of remembrances. The Lord bless you, my sweet wife, and all ours. Farewell.

Your faithful husband,

Jo. Winthrop.

Send not up my horses till I send for them.

On October 20, 1629, Winthrop was elected governor of the Massachusetts Bay Company. His days were then filled with organizing the Great Migration for the spring. His business again took him to London and away from Margaret.

October 20, 1629

My dear Wife,--I am very sorry that I am forced to feed you with letters, when my presence is your due, & so much desired. But my trust is that he who has so disposed of it, will supply you with patience, & better comfort in the want of him whom you so much desire. The Lord is able to do thus, & you may expect it, for he has promised it. Seeing he calls me into his work, he will have care of you & all ours & our affairs in my absence: therefore I must send you to him, for all you lack. Go boldly (sweet wife) to the throne of Grace. If anything troubles you, acquaint the Lord with it. Tell him, he has taken your husband from you, pray him to be a husband to you, a father to your children, a master to your household. You shall find him faithful. You are not guilty of my departure. You have not driven me away by any unkindness, or want of duty. Therefore, you may challenge protection and blessing of him.

I praise the Lord I am in health & cheerful in my course, wherein I find God graciously present, so as we expect, he will be pleased to direct and prosper us. We have great advantage because we have many prayers.

Be not discouraged (dear heart) though I set you no time of my return. I hope it shall not be long, & I will make no more stay than I needs must.

So it is that it has pleased the Lord to call me to a further trust in this business of the Plantation than either I expected or find myself fit for, (being chosen by the Company to be their Governor). The only thing that I have comfort of in it is, that in this I have the assurance that my charge is of the Lord, & that he has called me to this work. O that he would give me a heart now to answer his goodness to me, & the expectation of his people! I never had more need of prayers. Help me (dear wife) & let us set our hearts to seek the Lord, & cleave to him sincerely.

My brother and sisters salute you all. ... So the Lord bless you and all our children & company. So I kiss my sweet wife & rest

your faithful husband,
John Winthrop

My dear Husband,--I know not how to express my love to you or my desires of your wished welfare, but my heart is well known to you, which will make relation of my affections though they be small in appearance. My thoughts are now on our great change and alteration of our course here, which I beseech the Lord to bless us in, & my good Husband cheer up your heart in the expectation of God's goodness to us, & let nothing dismay or discourage you. If the Lord be with us, who can be against us?[34] My grief is the fear of staying behind you,[35] but I must leave all to the good providence of God. I thank the Lord we are all here in reasonable good health... thus with my best respect to yourself, brother & sister D[owning], I commit you to God and rest

Your faithful wife,
Margaret Winthrop.

---

34 Romans 8:31.

35 Margaret, who was pregnant, would not accompany John on the first voyage. John, Jr. stayed behind also to wrap up his father's affairs and take care of Margaret's passage.

January 31, 1630

My dear Wife,--I praise God, we came safe to London, and continue in health, and found all well here. Thus it pleases the Lord to follow us with his blessings, that we might love him again. I find here so much to do, as I doubt I shall not come down these three weeks. But, you may be sure, I will stay no longer than my occasions shall enforce me.

I must now begin to prepare you for our long parting, which grows very near. I know not how to deal with you by arguments. For if you were as wise and patient as ever woman was, yet it must needs be a great trial for you, and the greater, because I am so dear to you. That which I must chiefly look at in you, for a ground of contentment, is your godliness. If now the Lord be your God, you must show it by trusting in him, and resigning yourself quietly to his good pleasure. If now Christ be your Husband, you must show what sure and sweet intercourse is between him and your soul, when it shall be no hard thing for you to part with an earthly, mortal, infirm husband for his sake. The enlargement of your comfort in the communion of the love and sweet familiarity of your most holy, heavenly, and undefiled Lord and Husband, will abundantly recompense whatsoever want or inconvenience may come by the absence of the other. The best course is to turn all your reasons and discourse into prayers; for only he can help, who is Lord of sea and land, and has sole power of life and death.

It is now near eleven of the clock, and I shall write again ere long (if God will). The good Lord bless you and all your company. My brother and sister salute you all. Commend my hearty love to my good sister F[ones] and all the rest. ... So I kiss my sweet wife, and rest

Your frail, yet faithful husband,
Jo. Winthrop.

My dear Husband,--I received your sweet letter, and do bless God for all his mercy to us, in the continuance of your health and welfare, and the rest of us here. I am glad to hear you will come home this week, for I desire to enjoy your sweet presence as often as I can, before that long parting come which I desire the Lord to fit us for, and give me faith and patience to submit unto his will in all things which he requires at my hands. I trust he will sanctify it to me and give me a right use of it, that I may thereby learn the more to depend upon him. When other comforters fail me, he will supply the comfort of his Holy Spirit in the assurance of his love in Jesus Christ our Lord and Savior. I see your love to me and mine, my good Husband, is more than I can deserve, and you are more willing to grant then [sic] I forward to desire. The good Lord repay you all your kindness to me, but I will say no more of this till you come home. I beseech the Lord to send us a comfortable meeting, and thus with my best love to yourself, my brother and sister Downing, & all the rest of our friends, desire the Lord to send you a good end of all your troubles and enable you to go through them cheerfully, as I trust he will not fail you, into whose hands I commit you and rest

> your faithful and obedient wife,
> Margaret Winthrop

London, March 2, 1630.

Mine own dear Heart,--I must confess, you have overcome me with your exceeding great love, and those abundant expressions of it in your sweet letters, which savor of more than an ordinary spirit of love and piety. Blessed be the Lord our God, that gives strength and comfort to you to undergo this great trial, which, I must confess, would be too heavy for you, if the Lord did not put under his hand in so gracious a measure. Let this experience of his faithfulness to you in this first trial, be a ground to establish your heart to believe and expect his help in all that may follow. It grieves me much, that I lack time and freedom of mind to discourse with you (my faithful yoke fellow) in those things, which your sweet letters offer me so plentiful occasion for. I beseech the Lord, I may have liberty to supply it, before I depart, for I cannot thus leave you. Our two boys[36] and James Downing, John Samford and Mary M. and most of my servants, are gone this day towards South Hampton. The good Lord be with them and us all. Goodman Hawes was with me, and very kindly offers to bring his wife to Groton about the beginning of April, and so stay till yourself and my daughter[37] be in bed, so you shall not need take fare for a midwife. Ah, my most kind and dear wife, how sweet is your love to me! The Lord bless you and yours with the blessings from above and from beneath, of the right hand and the left, with plenty of favor and peace here, and eternal glory hereafter. All here are in health, (I praise God) and salute you. Remember my love and blessing to our children, and my salutations to all as you know. So I kiss and embrace you, and rest

Yours ever,

Jo. Winthrop.

Mine own, mine only, my best beloved,--Methinks it is very long since I saw or heard from my beloved, & I miss already the sweet comfort of your most desired presence. But the rich mercy & goodness of my God makes supply of all wants. Blessed be his great & holy name. Ah my good wife, we now find what blessing is stored up in the favor of the Lord.

---

36 Stephen and Adam. Henry also came to America on the voyage with his father, but he died in a drowning incident the day after his arrival. Of the other Winthrop children, Samuel stayed behind in England with Margaret. Forth was attending Cambridge and also stayed behind, though he fell ill and died in November of 1630. John, Jr. took care of Margaret and his father's estate until coming to America in 1631. Infant Ann died on the voyage over. Deane was left behind in school, but came over in 1635.

37 Henry's wife's daughter Martha was baptized at Groton on the following May 9.

He only sweetens all conditions to us, he takes our cares & fears from us. He supports us in our dangers; he disposes all our affairs for us; he will guide us by his counsel in our pilgrimage, & after will bring us to glory.[38]

John is returned from South Hampton, where he left our boys well & merry. This morning we are riding there, & from thence I shall take my last farewell of you till we meet in new England, or till midsummer that it please God our ships return. My dear wife be of good courage, it shall go well with you and us. The hairs of your head are numbered.[39] He who gave his only beloved to die for you, will give his Angels charge over you.[40] Therefore raise up your thoughts, & be merry in the Lord. Labor to live by your Faith. If you meet with troubles or difficulties, be not dismayed. God does use to bring his children into the straights of the Red Sea &c, that he may show his power and mercy in making a way for them. All his course towards us, are but to make us know him & love him. The more your heart draws towards him in this, the freer shall your condition be from the evil of Affliction...

Commend my hearty love to all our friends. I cannot now name them, but you know whom I mean. Now I beseech the Lord & father of mercy to bless you & all your company, my daughter W. Ma. Mat. Sam. Deane, & the little one unknown, Tho. Am.[41] & the rest. ... My dear wife farewell. Once again let us kiss and embrace, so in tears of great Affection I rest

Yours ever,
Jo. Winthrop.

From aboard the *Arabella*, riding at the Cowes, March 28, 1630.

---

38   Psalm 73:24.

39   Matthew 10:30.

40   Psalm 91:11.

41   The persons indicated by Tho. and Am. were undoubtedly his servants Thomas and Amy. The others, previously alluded to, were Henry's wife, his own daughter Mary, Martha Fones (afterwards the wife of his son John), and his sons Samuel and Deane.

To Mrs. Marg. Winthrop, the elder, at Groton.

My faithful and dear Wife,--It pleases God, that you should once again hear from me before our departure, and I hope this shall come safe to your hands. I know it will be a great refreshing to you. And blessed be his mercy, that I can write you so good news, that we are all in very good health, and, having tried our ship's entertainment now more than one week, we find it agree [sic] very well with us. Our boys are well and cheerful, and have no mind of home. They lie both with me, and sleep as soundly in a rug (for we use no sheets here) as ever they did at Groton, and so I do myself, (I praise God). The wind has been against us this week and more, but this day it is come fair to the north, so as we are preparing (by God's assistance) to set sail in the morning. We have only four ships ready, and some two or three Hollanders go along with us. The rest of our fleet (being seven ships) will not be ready this week. We have spent now two Sabbaths on shipboard very comfortably, (God be praised), and are daily more and more encouraged to look for the Lord's presence to go along with us. Henry Kingsbury has a child or two in the Talbot sick of the measles, but like to do well. One of my men had them at Hampton, but he was soon well again. We are, in all our eleven ships, about seven hundred persons, passengers, and two hundred and forty cows, and about sixty horses. The ship, which went from Plimouth, carried about one hundred and forty persons, and the ship, which goes from Bristol, carries about eighty persons. And now (my sweet soul) I must once again take my last farewell of you in Old England. It goes very near to my heart to leave you, but I know to whom I have committed you, even to him who loves you much better than any husband can, who has taken account of the hairs of your head, and puts all your tears in his bottle,[42] who can, and (if it be for his glory) will bring us

---

42   Psalm 56:8.

together again with peace and comfort. Oh, how it refreshes my heart, to think, that I shall yet again see your sweet face in the land of the living!--that lovely countenance, that I have so much delighted in, and behold with such great content! I have hitherto been so taken up with business, as I could seldom look back to my former happiness. But now, when I shall be at some leisure, I shall not avoid the remembrance of you, nor the grief of your absence. You have your share with me, but I hope the course we have agreed upon will be some ease to us both. Mondays and Fridays, at five of the clock at night, we shall meet in spirit till we meet in person. Yet, if all those hopes should fail, blessed be our God, that we are assured we shall meet one day, if not as husband and wife, yet in a better condition. Let that stay and comfort your heart. Neither can the sea drown your husband, nor enemies destroy, nor any adversity deprive you of your husband or children. Therefore I will take you now and my sweet children in my arms, and kiss and embrace you all, and so leave you with my God. Farewell, farewell. I bless you all in the name of the Lord Jesus. ... Pray all for us. Farewell. Commend my blessing to my son John. I cannot now write to him; but tell him I have committed you and yours to him. Labor to draw him yet nearer to God, and he will be the surer staff of comfort to you.

Yours wheresoever,
Jo. Winthrop.

Winthrop's two month voyage in the North Atlantic was a cold one. At one point, Winthrop delivered his now famous 'Modell of Christian Charity' aboard the *Arabella*, expressing what was to become the American dream - that the colony would be a 'city on a hill,' with the eyes of all people upon them. Winthrop saw the Puritan colonists as a chosen people working together in a new land to achieve God's will. As ships began to return to England, Winthrop took the opportunity to again write to Margaret.

To my very loving Wife, Mrs. Winthrop, the elder, at Groton, in Suffolk, near Sudbury. From New England.

Charleston in New England, July 16, 1630

My dear Wife,--Blessed be the Lord, our good God and merciful Father, that yet has preserved me in life and health to salute you, and to comfort your long longing heart with the joyful news of my welfare, and the welfare of your beloved children.

We had a long and troublesome passage, but the Lord made it safe and easy to us. Though we have met with many and great troubles, (as this bearer[43] can certify you,) yet he has pleased to uphold us, and to give us hope of a happy issue.

I am so overpressed with business, as I have no time for these or other mine private occasions. I only write now, that you may know, that yet I live and am mindful of you in all my affairs. The larger discourse of all things you shall receive from my brother Downing, which I must send by some of the last ships. We have met with many sad and discomfortable things, as you shall hear after, and the Lord's hand has been heavy upon myself in some very near to me. My son Henry! my son Henry! ah, poor child![44] Yet it grieves me much more for my dear daughter [Henry's wife in England]. The Lord strengthen and comfort her heart, to bear this cross patiently. I know you will not be wanting to her in this distress. Yet, for all these things, (I praise my God,) I am not discouraged, nor do I see cause to repent or despair of those good days here, which will make amends for all.

I shall expect you next summer, (if the Lord please,) and by that time I hope to be provided for your comfortable entertainment. My most sweet wife, be not disheartened.

---

43   Arthur Tyndal, Margaret's brother, came over with Winthrop and returned in the *Lion*, the first ship which returned.

44   Henry died in a drowning accident the day after his arrival in New England.

Trust in the Lord, and you shall see his faithfulness. Commend me heartily to all our kind friends at Castleins, Groton Hall, Mr. Leigh and his wife, my neighbor Cole, and all the rest of my neighbors and their wives, both rich and poor. ...

The good Lord be with you and bless you and all our children and servants. Commend my love to them all. I kiss and embrace you, my dear wife, and all my children, and leave you in his arms, who is able to preserve you all, and to fulfill our joy in our happy meeting in his good time. Amen

Your faithful husband,

J. Winthrop

Charleston in N. England July 23. 1630.

My dear Wife,--I wrote to you by my brother Arthur,[45] but I dare write no more then [sic] I need not care though it miscarried, for I found him the old man still. Yet I would have kept him to ease my brother, but that his own desire to return, and the scarcity of provisions here, yielded the stronger reason to let him go. Now (my good wife) let us join in praising our merciful God, that (howsoever he has afflicted us, both generally & particularly mine own family in his stroke upon my son Henry) yet myself & the rest of our children & family are safe & in health, & that he upholds our hearts that we faint not in all our troubles, but can wait for a good issue. Though our fare be but coarse in respect of what we formerly had, (peas, puddings & fish, being our ordinary diet), yet he makes it sweet & wholesome to us, that I may truly say I desire no better. Besides in this, that he begins with us in affliction, it is the greater argument to us of his love, & of the goodness of the work which we are about. For Satan bends his forces against us, & stirs up his instruments to all kind of mischief, so that

---

45   Arthur Tyndal was Margaret's brother who returned to England on the *Lion*.

I think here are some persons who never showed so much wickedness in England as they have done here. Therefore be not discouraged (my dear Wife) by anything you shall hear from here. You see (by our experience) that God can bring safe here even the tenderest women & the youngest children (as he did in many different ships, though the voyage were more tedious than formerly has been known in this season.) Be sure to be warm clothed, & to have store of fresh provisions, meal, eggs put up in salt or ground malt, butter, oat meal, peas, & fruits, & a large strong chest or 2, well locked to keep these provisions in. And be sure they are stowed in the ship where they be readily come by, (which the boatswain will see to & the quarter masters, if they be rewarded beforehand,) but for these things my son will take care. Be sure to have ready at sea 2 or 3 skillets of several sizes, a large frying pan, a small stewing pan, & a case to boil a pudding in, store of linen for use at sea, & sack [wine] to bestow among the sailors, some drinking vessels, & pewter & other vessels. And for medicine you shall need no other but a pound of Doctor Wright's Electuariu lenitivu, & his direction to use it, a gallon of scurvy grass to drink a little 5 or 6 mornings together, with some saltpeter dissolved in it, & a little grated or sliced nutmeg.

You must be sure to bring no more company then [sic] so many as shall have full provision for a year and a half, for though the earth here is fertile, yet there must be time & means to raise it. If we have corn enough we may live plentifully. Yet all these are but the means which God has ordained to do us good by. Our eyes must be towards him, who as he can withhold blessings from the strongest means, so he can give sufficient virtue to the weakest.

I am so straightened with much business, as can no way satisfy myself in writing to you. The Lord will in due time let us see the faces of each other again to our great comfort.

Now the Lord in mercy bless, guide & support you. I kiss & embrace you my dear wife. I kiss & bless you all my dear children, Forth, Mary, Deane, Sam, & the other. The Lord keep you all & work his true fear in your hearts. The blessing of the Lord be upon all my servants, whom salute from me, John, Samford, Amy &c, Goldston, Pease, Chote &c., my good friends at Castleins & all my good neighbors, Goodman Cole & his good wife, & all the rest.

Remember to come well furnished with linen, woolen, some more bedding, brass, pewter, leather bottles, drinking horns &c. Let my son provide 12 axes of several sorts of the Braintree Smith, or some other prime workman, whatever they cost, & some Augers great and small, & many other necessaries which I cannot now think of, as candles, soap, & store of beef suet, &c. Once again farewell my dear wife.

Your faithful husband,

John Winthrop.

September 9, 1630.

My dear Wife,--The blessing of God all-sufficient be upon you and all my dear ones with you forever.

I praise the good Lord, though we see much mortality, sickness, and trouble, yet (such is his mercy) myself and children, with most of my family, are yet living, and in health, and enjoy prosperity enough, if the affliction of our brethren did not hold under the comfort of it. The lady Arbella is dead, and good Mr. Higginson, my servant, old Waters of Neyland, and many others. Thus the Lord is pleased still to humble us. Yet he mixes so many mercies with his corrections, as we are persuaded he will not cast us off, but, in his due time, will do us good, according to the measure of our afflictions. He stays until he has purged our corruptions, and healed the hardness and error of our hearts, and stripped us of our vain confidence in this arm of flesh, that he may have us rely wholly upon himself.

The French ship, so long expected, and given for lost, is now come safe to us, about a fortnight since, having been twelve weeks at sea. Yet her passengers (being but few) all safe and well but one, and her goats but six living of eighteen. So as now we are somewhat refreshed with such goods and provisions as she brought, though much thereof has received damage by wet. I praise God, we have many occasions of comfort here, and do hope, that our days of affliction will soon have an end, and that the Lord will do us more good in the end than we could have expected. That will abundantly recompense for all the trouble we have endured. Yet we may not look at great things here. It is enough that we shall have heaven, though we should pass through hell to it. We here enjoy God and Jesus Christ. Is not this enough? What would we have more? I thank God, I like so well to be here, as I do not repent my coming, and if I were to come again, I would not have altered my course, though I had foreseen all these afflictions. I never fared better in my life, never slept better, never had more content of mind, which comes merely of the Lord's good hand, for we have not the like means of these comforts here, which we had in England. But the Lord is all-sufficient, blessed be his holy name. If he please, he can still uphold us in this estate. But, if he shall see good to make us partakers with others in more affliction, his will be done. He is our God, and may dispose of us as he sees good....

I long for the time, when I may see your sweet face again, and the faces of my dear children. But I must break off, and desire you to commend me kindly to all my good friends, and excuse my not writing at this time. If God please once to settle me, I shall make amends... The good Lord bless you and all our children and family. So I kiss my sweet wife and my dear children and rest

Your faithful husband,
John Winthrop.

About mid-August, 1631, Margaret Winthrop, with her infant daughter Ann and John, Jr., embarked on the *Lion* for New England. Little Ann died a week after the voyage began. Minister John Eliot, later famous for his missionary work among the Indians, was also on board the ship and undoubtedly gave much spiritual comfort to the Winthrops. After ten weeks at sea, the ship arrived in New England, and most of the people in the area came out to welcome the governor's wife and family. As John wrote in his journal, the people 'brought and sent, for many days, great store of provisions, as fat hogs, kids, venison, poultry, geese, partridges, &c., so as the like joy and manifestation of love had never been seen in New England. It was a great marvel, that so much people & such store of provision could be gathered together at so few hours' warning.'[46] The next week the colony kept a day of thanksgiving at Boston.

Margaret and John lived together in Boston for fifteen years, undoubtedly at the head of society there. Their strong spiritual union had only grown stronger through their years of separation and difficulties. In 1647, an epidemic swept through the colony. Margaret Winthrop fell sick June 13 and died the next morning. John wrote in his diary

> June 14. In this sickness the governor's wife, daughter of Sir John Tindal, knight, left this world for a better, being about fifty-six years of age; a woman of singular virtue, prudence, modesty, and specially beloved and honored of all the country.[47]

At the beginning of 1648, Winthrop married a fourth time, to widow Martha Coytmore. He died at the age of 62, on March 26, 1649.

---

46 *Life and Letters of John Winthrop*, Vol. II, 90.
47 *Life and Letters of John Winthrop*, Vol. II, 362.

HENRY MARTYN

AND

LYDIA GRENFELL

Henry Martyn	Lydia Grenfell
(1781-1812)	(1775-1829)

'Oh, my beloved sister and friend, dear to me on every account,
but dearest of all for having one heart and one soul with me in the
cause of Jesus and the love of God.'
Henry Martyn

Henry Martyn, one of the early English missionaries to India, died when only 31. Like the American missionary David Brainerd, whose zeal lit Martyn's own fire for missions, Henry was totally devoted to the cause of Christ and willing to 'burn out' for Christ if necessary. While at Cambridge University and attending the Trinity Church pastored by Rev. Charles Simeon, Henry learned of the great results that had come from the work of William Carey, who had gone to India as a missionary ten years previously, in 1792.

Because he needed to support a younger sister, Henry was unable to go to India with the financial uncertainties of a missionary to the Indian natives, but he was able to fulfill the missionary call by becoming a chaplain in the East India Company. In this way he could support his sister by ministering to the English in India while also developing a ministry among the native peoples.

When Henry departed England in 1805, he left behind many friends and family members. Most difficult was leaving behind Lydia Grenfell, a young lady in Cornwall with whom Henry had developed a deep attachment and spiritual rapport. Lydia had been engaged to Mr Samuel John, a lawyer of Penzance, but he had broken off the engagement and planned to marry someone else. Mr John, however, did not finally marry until 1810, and Lydia still felt in some way bound to him because she had given her word. Though Henry declared his affections for Lydia before he went to India, she would not bind herself or him to any commitment. She was reluctant to reveal to Henry the depth of her affection for him; she wanted him to be free to marry in India if he chose, without being bound to her. Each struggled with a love for the other while wanting to be solely devoted to the Lord and His service.

While at the coast, Martyn's ship was delayed, and he managed to spend a few more days with his friends in Cornwall. Lydia's diary entries during this time reveal something of the struggle of her soul:

August 8.--I was surprised again to -day by a visit from my friend, Mr. Martyn, who, contrary to every expectation, is detained, perhaps weeks longer. I feel myself called on to act decisively--oh how difficult and painful a part--Lord, assist me. I desire to be directed by Thy wisdom, and to follow implicitly what appears Thy will. May we each consider Thy honour as entrusted to us, and resolve, whatever it may cost us, to seek Thy glory and do Thy will. Oh Lord, I feel myself so weak that I would fain fly from the trial. My hope is in Thee--do thou strengthen me, help me to seek, to know, and resolutely to do, Thy will, and that we may be each divinely influenced, and may principle be victorious over feeling. Thou, blessed Spirit, aid, support, and guide us. Now may we be in the armour of God, now may we flee from temptation. O blessed Jesus, leave me not, forsake me not.[1]

1 George Smith, *Henry Martyn, Saint and Scholar.* New York: Fleming H. Revell Co., n.d., 91.

Dedicating himself totally to the Lord's service, Henry Martyn determined to set his affections on things above, and not on things on the earth. He parted from Lydia with 'a sort of uncertain pain, which I knew would increase to greater violence.'[2] He looked to eternity when he knew he could again enjoy Lydia's company in the presence of Christ. Even so, when Henry Martyn left England, he shed tears and

> thought of the roaring seas, which would soon be rolling between me and all that is dear to me on earth. ... My feelings were those of a man who should suddenly be told, that every friend he had in the world was dead. It was only by prayer for them that I should be comforted; and this was indeed a refreshment to my soul, because by meeting them at the throne of grace, I seemed to be again in their society.[3]

The trip to India took nine months - July, 1805 to April, 1806. The *Union* stopped at St. Salvador and Cape of Good Hope on its way to India. Henry's first months in India were spent among the English at Calcutta and Serampore. Though he anticipated being assigned to a post farther inland, once Henry had assessed conditions in India, he began to believe it possible to marry Lydia and fulfill his missionary call to India. Friends in India as well as in England encouraged Martyn to marry. Accordingly, Henry's first letter to Lydia from India was his marriage proposal.[4]

---

2   John Sargent, *The Life and Letters of Henry Martyn*. Edinburgh: The Banner of Truth Trust, 1985 edition of 1862, 66.

3   *Life and Letters of Henry Martyn*, 86, 91.

4   Letters from Henry Martyn to Miss Grenfell are from John Sargent, *The Life and Letters of Henry Martyn*, Edinburgh: The Banner of Truth Trust, 1985 edition of 1862, Appendix. Additional information about Lydia and Henry Martyn can be found in Barbara Eaton's *Letters to Lydia*. Penzance, UK: Hypatia Publications Ltd., 2005. Besides additional biographical information about Lydia and Henry, Eaton includes a chapter on the nineteenth-century fictional works and novels which the letters between the two influenced, including Harriet Parr's *Her Title of Honour*, Mary Sherwood's *Little Henry and His Bearer*, and Charlotte Brontë's *Jane Eyre*.

Serampore,[5] July 30, 1806.

My dearest Lydia

On a subject so intimately connected with my happiness and future ministry, as that on which I am now about to address you, I wish to assure you that I am not acting with precipitancy, or without much consideration and prayer; while I at last sit down to request you to come out to me in India.

May the Lord graciously direct His blind and erring creature, and not suffer the natural bias of his mind to lead him astray. You are acquainted with much of the conflict I have undergone on your account. It has been greater than you ... have imagined, and yet not so painful as I deserve to have found it, for having suffered my affections to fasten so inordinately on an earthly object.

Soon, however, after my final departure from Europe, God in great mercy gave me deliverance and favoured me throughout the voyage with peace of mind, indifference about all worldly connections, and devotedness to no object upon earth but the work of Christ. I gave you up entirely - not the smallest expectation remained in my mind of ever seeing you again till we should meet in heaven: and the thought of this separation was the less painful from the consolatory persuasion that our own Father had so ordered it for our mutual good. I continued from that time to remember you in my prayers only as a Christian sister, though one very dear to me. On my arrival in this country I saw no reason at first for supposing that marriage was advisable for a missionary - or rather the subject did not offer itself to my mind. The Baptist missionaries[6] indeed recommended

---

5   Serampore, located sixteen miles from Calcutta, was the site of a Danish colony which also became the center of operations for the English Baptist missionaries. The East India Company would not allow missionaries to minister in British India.

6   The Baptist mission in India was established by William Carey in 1793. In 1799 Carey was joined by Joshua Marshman and William Ward. Because of the British East India Company's prohibition against missionaries, the Baptist missionaries worked out of the Danish colony of Serampore. Carey was delighted with Henry Martyn when he met him and declared that wherever Martyn was, no other missionary would be needed.

it, and Mr. Brown;[7] but not knowing any proper person in this country, they were not very pressing upon the subject, and I accordingly gave no attention to it. After a very short experience and inquiry afterwards, my own opinions began to change, and when a few weeks ago we received your welcome letter, and others from Mr. Simeon[8] and Colonel Sandys, both of whom spoke of you in reference to me, I considered it even as a call from God to satisfy myself fully concerning his will. From the account which Mr. Simeon received of you from Mr. Thomason,[9] he seemed in his letter to me to regret that he had so strongly dissuaded me from thinking about you at the time of my leaving England. Colonel Sandys spoke in such terms of you, and of the advantages to result from your presence in this country, that Mr. B.[rown] became very earnest for me to endeavour to prevail upon you. Your letter to me perfectly delighted him, and induced him to say that you would be the greatest aid to the Mission I could possibly meet with. I knew my own heart too well not to be distrustful of it, especially as my affections were again awakened, and accordingly all my labour and prayer have been directed to check their influence, that I might see clearly the path of duty.

---

7   David Brown (1763-1812) first came to India in 1786 as a chaplain to the brigade at Fort William in Calcutta. For the rest of his life he devoted himself to the cause of Christian missions in India, both of the Church of England and other denominations. A Hebrew scholar, he established a translation library in Bengal and encouraged Bible translation into the many languages of the Orient. When Henry Martyn arrived in India, Brown welcomed him into his home, and the two became intimate friends. During the five months Martyn was waiting for his appointment, he stayed at Aldeen House in Serampore with Brown and his family, living in an ancient idol temple in the garden. Ever after the building was known as 'Henry Martyn's Pagoda'.

8   Henry Martyn had been a curate of Charles Simeon (1759-1836), evangelical pastor of Holy Trinity, Cambridge. When Charles Grant, a director of the East India Company, sought to establish Christian missions in India with government support and protection, Simeon became his confidential advisor in the appointment of chaplains. Some of Simeon's most capable curates became chaplains of the East India Company. Simeon continued his correspondence with Martyn until Martyn's death.

9   Thomas Truebody Thomason was a curate of Charles Simeon and an intimate friend of Henry Martyn. In 1808 Thomason accepted a chaplaincy in Bengal and followed Martyn to India.

Though I dare not say that I am under no bias, yet from every view of the subject I have been able to take, after balancing the advantages and disadvantages that may ensue to the cause in which I am engaged, always in prayer for God's direction, my reason is fully convinced of the expediency, I had almost said the necessity of having you with me. It is possible that my reason may still be obscured by passion; let it suffice however to say that now, with a safe conscience and the enjoyment of the Divine presence, I calmly and deliberately make the proposal to you - and blessed be God if it be not His will to permit it; still this step is not advancing beyond the limits of duty, because there is a variety of ways by which God can prevent it, without suffering any dishonour to his cause. If He shall forbid it, I think, that be his grace, I shall even then be contented, and rejoice in the pleasure of corresponding with you.

Your letter dated December, 1805, was the first I received, and I found it so animating that I could not but reflect on the blessedness of having so dear a counselor always near me. I can truly say, and God is my witness, that my principal desire in this affair is, that you may promote the kingdom of God in my own heart, and be the means of extending it to the heathen. My own earthly comfort and happiness are not worth a moment's notice. I would not, my dearest Lydia, influence you by any artifices or false representations. I can only say that if you have a desire of being instrumental in establishing the blessed Redeemer's kingdom among these poor people, and will condescend to do it by supporting the spirits and animating zeal of a weak messenger of the Lord who is apt to grow very dispirited and languid, 'Come, and the Lord be with you!' It can be nothing but a sacrifice on your part, to leave your valuable friends to come to one who is utterly unworthy of you or any other of God's precious gifts - but you will have your reward, and I ask it not of you or of God for the sake of my own happiness, but only on account of the Gospel. If it be not calculated to promote it, may God in his mercy withhold it. For the satisfaction of your friends, I should say, that you will meet with no hardships. The voyage is very agreeable, and with the people and country of India I think you will be pleased. The climate is very fine - the so-much dreaded heat is really nothing to those who will employ their minds in useful pursuits. Idleness will make people complain of everything. The natives are the most harmless and timid creatures I ever met with. The whole country is the land of plenty and peace. Were I a missionary among the Esquimaux or Boschemen [sic] I should never dream of introducing a female into such a scene of danger or hardship, especially one whose happiness is dearer to me than my own, - but here there is universal tranquillity [sic], - though the multitudes are so great, that a missionary needs not go three miles from his house to find a congregation of many thousands. You would not be left in solitude if I were to make any distant excursion; because no chaplain is stationed where there is not a large English society. My salary is abundantly sufficient for the support of a married man; the house and number of people kept by each Company's servant being such as to need no increase for a family establishment.

As I must make the supposition of your coming, though it may be perhaps a premature liberty, I should give you some directions. This letter will reach you about the latter end of the year, - it would be very desirable if you could be ready for the February fleet, because the voyage will be performed in far less time than at any other season. George[10] will find out the best ship; one in which there is a lady of high rank in the service would be preferable. You are to be considered as coming as a visitor to Mr. Brown, who will write to you or to Colonel Sandys, who is best qualified to give you directions about the voyage. Should I be up the country on your arrival in Bengal, Mr. Brown will be at hand to receive you, and you will find yourself immediately at home. As it will highly expedite some of the plan we have in agitation that you should know the language as soon as possible, take Gilchrist's *Indian Stranger's Guide*, and occasionally on the voyage learn some of the words.

If I had room I might enlarge on much that would be interesting to you. In my conversations with Marshman, the Baptist missionary, our hearts sometimes expand with delight and joy at the prospect of seeing all these nations of the East receive the doctrine of the Cross. He is a happy labourer: and I only wait, I trust, to know the language to open my mouth boldly and make known the mystery of the Gospel. My romantic notions are for the first time almost realized, --for in addition to the beauties of sylvan scenery may be seen the more delightful object of multitudes of simple people sitting in the shade, listening to the words of eternal life. Much as yet is not done but I have seen many discover by their looks while Marshman was preaching, that their hearts were tenderly affected. My post is not yet determined; we expect however it will be Patna, a civil station, where I shall not be under military command. As you are so kindly anxious about my health, I am happy to say, that through mercy my health is far better than it ever was in England. ...

However you shall decide, my dearest Lydia, I *must* approve your determination, because with that spirit of simple looking to the Lord, which we both endeavour to maintain, we must not doubt that you will be divinely directed. Till I receive an answer to this, my prayers, you may be assured, will be constantly put up for you, that in this affair you may be under an especial guidance, and that in all your ways

God may be abundantly glorified by you through Jesus Christ. You say in your letter that *frequently every day* you remember my worthless name before the throne of grace. This instance of extraordinary and undeserved kindness draws my heart toward you with a tenderness which I cannot describe. Dearest Lydia, in the sweet and fond expectation of your being given to me by God, and of the happiness which I humbly hope you yourself might enjoy here, I find pleasure in breathing out my assurance of ardent love. I have now long loved you most affectionately, and my attachment is more strong, more pure, more heavenly, because I see in you the image of Jesus Christ. I unwillingly conclude, by bidding my beloved Lydia adieu.

H. MARTYN

Serampore, Sept. 1, 1806

My Dearest Lydia,

With this you will receive the duplicate of the letter I sent you a month ago by the Overland Despatch. May it find you prepared to come! All the thoughts and views which I have had of the subject since first addressing you, add tenfold confirmation to my first opinion; and I trust that the blessed God will graciously make it appear that I have been acting under a right direction, by giving the precious gift to me and to the Church in India. ... It is a consolation to me during this long suspense, that had I engaged with you before my departure I should not have had such a satisfactory conviction of it being the will of God. The Commander-in-Chief is in doubt to which of the three following stations he shall appoint me, --Benares, Patna, or Moorshedabad; it will be the last most probably; this is only two days' journey from Calcutta; I shall take my departure in about six weeks. ... I am very happy here in preparing for my delightful work; but I should be happier still if I were sufficiently fluent in the language to be actually employed; and happiest of all if my beloved Lydia were at my right hand, counseling and animating me. I am not very willing to end my letter to you; it is difficult not to prolong the enjoyment of speaking, as it were, to one who occupies so much of my sleeping and waking hours; but here, alas! I am aware of danger; and my dear Lydia will, I hope, pray that her unworthy friend may love no creature so inordinately.

It will be base in me to depart in heart from a God of such love as I find him to be. Oh, that I could make some returns for the riches of his love! Swiftly fly the hours of life away, and then we shall be admitted to behold his glory. The ages of darkness are rolling fast away, and shall soon usher in the gospel period, when the whole world shall be filled with his glory. Oh, my beloved sister and friend, dear to me on every account, but dearest of all for having one heart and one soul with me in the cause of Jesus and the love of God, let us pray and rejoice, and rejoice and pray, that God may be glorified, and the dying Savior see of the travail of his soul. May the God of hope fill us with all joy and peace in believing, that we may both of us abound in hope through the power of the Holy Ghost. Now, my dearest Lydia, I cannot say what I feel--I cannot pour out my soul--I could not if you were here; but I pray that you may love me, if it be the will of God; and I pray that God may make you more and more his Child, and give me more and more love for all that is Godlike and holy.

I remain, with fervent affection.

Yours, in eternal bonds,
H. MARTYN.

Serampore, Sept. 1806.
How earnestly do I long for the arrival of my dearest Lydia! Though it may prove at last no more than a waking dream

that I ever expected to receive you in India, the hope is too pleasing not to be cherished till I am forbidden any longer to hope. Till I am assured of the contrary, I shall find a pleasure in addressing you as my own. If you are not to be mine, you will pardon me; but my expectations are greatly encouraged by the words you used when we parted at Gurlyn, that I had better *go out* free; implying, as I thought, that you would not be unwilling to follow me if I should see it to be the will of God to make the request. I was rejoiced also to see in your letter that you unite your name with mine, when you pray that God would keep us both in the path of duty; from this I infer that you are by no means *determined* to remain separate from me. You will not suppose, my dear Lydia, that I mention these little things to influence your conduct, or to implicate you in an engagement. --No, I acknowledge that you are perfectly free, and I have no doubt that you will act as the love and wisdom of our God shall direct. Your heart is far less interested in this business than mine, in all probability; and this on one account I do not regret, as you will be able to see more clearly the directions of God's providence. ... Yet how will my dear sister Emma[11] be able to part with you and George--but, above all, your *mother*? I feel very much for you and for them, but I have no doubt at all about your health and happiness in this country.

The Commander-in-Chief has at last appointed me to the station of Dinapore, near Patna,[12] and I shall accordingly take my departure for that place as soon as I can make the necessary preparations. It is not exactly the situation I wished for--though, in a temporal point of view, it is desirable enough.

---

11 Emma was actually Lydia's sister. She had married Rev. T. Martyn Hitchins, Martyn's cousin. Martyn's correspondence with Emma shows he easily expressed his deepest thoughts and feelings with her, making her a confidante in his affections for Lydia

12 Patna, one of India's most ancient cities and an early Buddhist capital, is located on the Ganges about 300 miles northwest of Calcutta. It was the second city in Bengal after Calcutta and the fifth largest in all India, with a population of half a million.

The air is good, the living cheap, the salary of £1000 a year, and there is a large body of English troops there. But I should have preferred being near Benares, the heart of Hinduism. We rejoice to hear that two other brethren are arrived at Madras on their way to Bengal, sent, I trust, by the Lord, to co-operate in overturning the kingdom of Satan in these regions. They are Corrie[13] and Parsons, both Bengal chaplains. Their stations will be Benares and Moorshedabad--one on one side of me, and the other on the other. There are also now ten Baptist missionaries at Serampore. Surely good is intended for this country!

Captain Wickes,--the good old Captain Wickes, who has brought out so many missionaries to India, is now here. He reminds me of Uncle S___. I have just been interrupted by the blaze of a funeral pile, within a hundred yards of my pagoda; I ran out, but the wretched woman had consigned herself to the flames before I reached the spot, and I saw only the remains of her and her husband.[14] O Lord, how long shall it be? Oh! I shall have no rest in my spirit till my tongue is loosed to testify against the devil, and deliver the message of God to these his unhappy bond-slaves. I stammered out something to the wicked Brahmins[15] about the judgments of God upon them for the murder they had just committed, but they said it was an act of her own free will. Some of the missionaries would have been there, but they are forbidden by the Governor-General to preach to

---

13 Daniel Corrie (1777-1837), also a protegé of Cambridge's Charles Simeon, was appointed to a chaplaincy in Bengal in 1806. Corrie met Martyn in Calcutta at the home of David Brown, and the two became intimate friends. Like Martyn, Corrie did missionary work among the Indians in addition to serving as chaplain to British troops. Corrie served in India for thirty years and was appointed bishop of Madras a year before his death.

14 Under the practice of sati (or suttee), wifely devotion to her husband was to continue into the grave. Widows were placed on the funeral pyres and cremated alive with the bodies of their dead husbands. The practice also solved the economic problems of caring for widows. Sati horrified the Western missionaries. William Carey especially worked for its abolition, and in 1829 the British government abolished the practice. In remote regions, however, sati deaths continued to be reported into the twentieth century.

15 Brahmins were the highest caste of the Hindus and usually were Hindu priests.

the natives in the British territory.[16] Unless this prohibition is revoked by an order from home, it will amount to a total suppression of the Mission.

... Continue to remember me in your prayers, as a weak brother. I shall always think of you as one to be loved and honoured.

H. MARTYN.

Martyn's formal proposal reached Lydia March 2, 1807. Though her affections and sympathies were inextricably drawn to Henry's, she felt strongly that having promised to marry S. John she was not free to marry another.

Rev. Simeon counseled Lydia to marry Martyn. She, however, wasn't sure of her health, the propriety of going to India alone to get married, her freedom to marry when Mr John was still unmarried, or of her mother's permission. Rev. Simeon was able to deal with all her objections except her mother's attitude and said that must be a matter of prayer. Lydia sent Martyn a refusal in her mother, Mrs Grenfell's, name.

While awaiting Lydia's answer, Henry continued thinking of Lydia. One night he dreamed Lydia had arrived in India, but he awoke to find this not true. His diary reflects his intense love for Lydia struggling with his love for God:

> December 23 [1806].--Had no freedom or power in prayer, though some appearance of tenderness. Lydia is a snare to me; I think of her so incessantly, and with such foolish and extravagant fondness, that my heart is drawn away from God. Though at night, can that be true love which is other than God would have it? No; that which is lawful is most genuine when regulated by the holy law of God.[17]

---

16   The East India Company would not allow missionaries into the British provinces. The Company feared that missionaries would upset business and cause unrest among the native population by attacking the native customs and religion as they preached the gospel. Largely through the prodding of William Wilberforce and the Clapham Sect, in 1813 Parliament passed the Charter Act, allowing missionaries into India.

17   *Henry Martyn, Saint and Scholar*, 209.

When Martyn received Lydia's refusal of marriage, he was severely disappointed, but sought to focus anew on the grace of God and his service to Him.

Dinapore, Oct. 24, 1807

MY DEAR LYDIA,

Though my heart is bursting with grief and disappointment, I write not to blame you. The rectitude of your conduct secures you from censure. Permit me calmly to reply to your letter of March 5, which I have just received.

You condemn yourself for having given me, though unintentionally, encouragement to believe that my attachment was returned. Perhaps you have. I have read your former letters with feelings less sanguine since the receipt of the last, and I am still not surprised at the interpretation I put upon them. But why accuse yourself for having written in this strain? It has not increased my expectations, nor consequently embittered my disappointment. When I addressed you in my first letter on the subject, I was not induced to it by any appearances of regard you had expressed; neither at any subsequent period have my hopes of your consent been founded on a belief of your attachment to me. I knew that your conduct would be regulated, not by personal feelings, but by a sense of duty. And therefore you have nothing to blame yourself for on this head.

In your last letter you do not assign, among your reasons for refusal, a want of regard to me. In that case I could not in decency give you any further trouble. On the contrary you say that '*present* circumstances seem to you to forbid my indulging expectations.' As this leaves an opening, I presume to address you again; and till the answer arrives, must undergo another eighteen months of torturing suspense.[18]

---

18   It took nine months to travel to India. Sending a letter and receiving a reply would take at least eighteen months.

Alas, my rebellious heart! what a tempest agitates me! I knew not that I had made so little progress in a spirit of resignation to the Divine will. I am in my chastisement like the bullock unaccustomed to the yoke, like a wild bull in a net, full of the fury of the Lord, the rebuke of my God. The death of my late most beloved sister almost broke my heart; but I hoped it had softened me, and made me willing to suffer.[19] But now my heart is as though destitute of the grace of God, full of misanthropic disgust with the world, and sometimes feeling resentment against yourself and Emma, and Mr. Simeon, and, in short, all whom I love and honour most. Sometimes in pride and anger resolving to write neither to you nor to any one else again. These are the motions of sin. My love and my better reason draw me to you again.

But now, with respect to your mother, I confess that the chief, and indeed only difficulty lies here. Considering that she is *your* mother, as I hoped she would be mine, and that her happiness depends so much on you; considering also that I am God's minister, which, amidst all the tumults of my soul I dare not forget, I falter in beginning to give advice which may prove contrary to the law of God. God forbid, therefore, that I should say, disobey your parents where the Divine law does not command you to disobey them; neither do I positively take upon myself to say that this is a case in which the law of God requires you to act in contradiction to them. I would rather suggest to your mother some considerations which justify me in attempting to deprive her of the company of a beloved child.

26th. A Sabbath having intervened since the above was written, I find myself more tranquilized by the sacred exercises

---

19 Henry's oldest sister died after a brief illness. Though comforted by assurance of her salvation, Henry wrote that 'her departure has left this world a frightful blank to me; and I feel not the smallest wish to live, except there be some work assigned for me to do in the church of God.'

of the day. One passage of Scripture which you quote has been much on my mind, and I find it very appropriate and decisive, -that we are not to 'make ourselves crooked paths, which whoso walketh in shall not know peace' [Isaiah 59:8]. Let me say I must be therefore contented to wait till you feel that the way is clear. But I intended to justify myself to Mrs. Grenfell. Let her not suppose that I would make her, or any other of my fellow-creatures miserable, that I might be happy. If there were no reason for your coming here, and the contest were only between Mrs. Grenfell and me, that is, between her happiness and mine, I would urge nothing further, but resign you to her. But I have considered that there are many things that might reconcile her to a separation from you (if indeed a separation is necessary, for if she would come along with you, I should rejoice the more). First, she does not depend on you alone for the comfort of her declining years. She is surrounded by friends. She has a greater number of sons and daughters honourably established in the world, than fall to the lot of most parents - all of whom would be happy having her amongst them. Again, if a person worthy of your hand, and settled in England, were to offer himself, Mrs. G. would not have insuperable objections, though it *did* deprive her of a daughter. ...

Your mother cannot be so misinformed respecting India and the voyage to it, as to be apprehensive on account of the clime or passage, in these days, when multitudes of ladies every year, with constitutions as delicate as yours, go to and fro in perfect safety, and a vastly greater majority enjoy their health here than in England. With respect to my means, I need add nothing to what was said in my first letter. But alas! what is my affluence good for now? It never gave me pleasure, but when I thought you were to share it with me. Two days ago I was hastening on the alterations in my house and garden, supposing you were at hand; but now every object excites disgust. My wish upon the whole is, that if you perceive it would be your duty to come to India, were it not for your mother, - and of that you cannot doubt, - supposing, I mean, that your inclinations are indifferent, then you should make me acquainted with your thoughts, and let us leave it to God how He will determine her mind. ...

Day and night I cease not to pray for you, though I fear my prayers are of little value. But as an encouragement to you to pray, I cannot help transcribing a few words from my journal, written at the time you wrote your letter to me. (7th March.) 'On the two last days (you wrote your letter on the 5th), felt no desire for a comfortable settlement in the world, scarcely any pleasure at the thought of Lydia's coming, except so far as her being sent might be for the good of my soul, and assistance to my work.' How manifestly is there an omnipresent, all-seeing God, and how sure we may be that prayers for spiritual blessings are heard by our God and Father! Oh, let that endearing name quell every murmur! When I am sent for, to different parts of the country to officiate at marriages, I sometimes think, amidst the festivity of the company, Why does all go so easily with them, and so hardly with me? They come together without difficulty, and I am balked and disconcerted almost every step I take, and condemned to wear away the time in uncertainty. Then I call to mind that to live without chastening is allowed to the spurious offspring; while to suffer is the privilege of the children of God.

Dearest Lydia, must I conclude? I could prolong my communion with you through many sheets; how many things I have to say to you, which I hoped to have communicated in person! But the more I write and the more I think of you, the more my affection warms, and I should feel it difficult to keep my pen from expressions that might not be acceptable to you.

Farewell! dearest, most beloved Lydia. Remember your faithful and ever affectionate,

H. MARTYN.

In his journal, Henry Martyn expressed the prayer of his heart that Lydia's refusal of marriage would stir him to greater devotion and service for the Lord:

> The Lord sanctify this; and since this last desire of my heart is also withheld, may I turn away for ever from the world, and henceforth live, forgetful of all but God. With Thee, O my God, is no disappointment. I shall never have to 'regret that I have loved Thee too well. Thou has said, 'Delight thyself in the Lord, and he shall give thee the desires of thy heart'[20]
>
> At first I was more grieved at the loss of my gourd, than for all the perishing Ninevehs around me; but now my earthly woe and earthly attachments seem to be absorbing in the vast concern of communicating the Gospel to these nations.[21] After this last lesson from God, on the vanity of the creature, I feel desirous of nothing, to have nothing, to ask for nothing, but what He gives.[22]

At Dinapore Martyn not only ministered to the English stationed there, but he also began an important work among the natives. At his own expense he began five schools around Dinapore. He translated the *Book of Common Prayer* into Hindostanee and began worship services for the natives in that language, though he did not yet feel capable to preach in the native tongues. Martyn also diligently worked on translations of the New Testament into Hindostanee, Persian, and Arabic.

---

20   Psalm 37:4.

21   After the prophet Jonah preached to the people of Nineveh, he was more concerned about his own comfort when a gourd protecting him from the sun died, than with the eternal plight of his Ninevite audience.

22   *Life and Letters of Henry Martyn*, 228-229.

In 1809 Martyn was transferred to the station at Cawnpore, four hundred miles northwest of Dinapore and even further from Calcutta and his friends Daniel Corrie and David Brown. Though the long journey in intense heat had further weakened Martyn's health, at Cawnpore he continued active in the same ministries and works he had at Dinapore. He also began to preach to the natives in their own language for the first time, though often interrupted and attacked physically.

Afflictions continued to buffet Martyn. He himself suffered from consumption or tuberculosis, the disease which had already taken his parents and oldest sister. Now he learned that his youngest sister, who had been instrumental in his own conversion, painfully died of the same disease. All of Martyn's family, his parents, brother, and two sisters, were now dead. Mercifully, Lydia wrote to Henry offering to take the place of a sister to him. She undoubtedly now felt a freedom in writing to Henry because of Mr John's marriage. Her diary records:

> January 24, 1810.--Heard yesterday of the marriage of Mr. John--what a mercy to me do I feel it!--a load gone off my mind, for every evil I heard of his committing I feared I might have been the cause of, by my conduct ten years since--I rejoice in this event for his sake and my own.
>
> February 6.--Heard at last of the safety of my friend in India, and wrote to him--many fears on my mind as to its propriety, and great deadness of soul in doing it--yet ere I concluded I felt comforted from the thought of the nearness of eternity, and the certainty that then, without any fear of doing wrong, I should again enjoy communion with him.[23]

Henry gratefully replied to Lydia's renewed correspondence:

---

23 *Henry Martyn, Saint and Scholar*, 300.

Cawnpore, March 30, 1810

Since you kindly bid me, my beloved friend, to consider you in place of that dear sister, whom it has pleased God in his wisdom to take from me, I gratefully accept the offer of a correspondence, which it has ever been the anxious wish of my heart to establish. Your kindness is the more acceptable, because it is shown in the day of affliction. Though I had heard of my dearest sister's illness, some months before I received the account of her death, and though the nature of her disorder was such as left me not a ray of hope, so that I was mercifully prepared for the event, still the certainty of it fills me with anguish. It is not that she has left me, for I never expected to see her more on earth. I have no doubt of meeting her in heaven, but I cannot bear to think of the pangs of dissolution she underwent, which have been unfortunately detailed to me with too much particularity. Would that I had never heard them, or could efface them from my remembrance! But oh, may I learn what the Lord is teaching me by these repeated strokes. May I learn meekness and resignation. May the world always appear as vain as it does now, and my continuance in it as short and uncertain. How frightful is the desolation which Death makes, and how appalling his visits when he enters one's family! I would rather never have been born, though be born to die, were it not for Jesus, the Prince of Life, the resurrection and the life. How inexpressibly precious is this Saviour, when eternity seems near! I hope often to communicate with you on these subjects, and in return for your kind and consolatory letters, to send you, from time to time, accounts of myself and my proceedings. Through you, I can hear of all my friends in the West. When I first heard of the loss I was likely to suffer, and began to reflect on my own friendless situation, you were much in my thoughts, -- whether you would be silent on this occasion or no? whether you would persist in your resolution? Friends indeed I have,

and brethren, blessed be God! but two brothers cannot supply
the place of one sister. When month after month passed away,
and no letter came from you, I almost abandoned the hope
of ever hearing from you again. It only remained to wait the
result of my last application through Emma. You have kindly
anticipated my request, and, I need scarcely add, are more
endeared to me than ever.

Of your illness, my dearest Lydia, I had heard nothing,
and it was well for me that I did not.

Yours most affectionately,

H. MARTYN.

Cawnpore, April 19, 1810

I begin my correspondence with my beloved Lydia, not
without a fear of its being soon to end. Shall I venture
to tell you, that our family complaint [consumption or
tuberculosis] has again made its appearance in me, with
more unpleasant symptoms than it has ever yet done?
However, God, who two years ago redeemed my life from
destruction, may again, for his Church's sake, interpose for
my deliverance.[24] Though alas! what am I, that my place
should not instantly be supplied by far more efficient
instruments? The symptoms I mentioned are chiefly a pain
in the chest, occasioned, I suppose, by over-exertion the
two last Sundays, and incapacitating me at present from all
public duty and even from conversation. You were mistaken
in supposing that my former illness originated from study.
Study never makes me ill--scarcely ever fatigues me--but
my lungs! death is seated there; it is speaking that kills me.
May it give others life! 'Death worketh in us, but life in
you' [2 Cor. 4:12]. Nature intended me, as I should judge

24   At Dinapore, in 1808, Martyn fainted and was in such weakness when he came to, that
he felt certain death was near. He had enough strength to make his will and thought
comfortably of the eternity he would soon enter. He amazingly recovered, however, and his
entrance into eternity was postponed.

from the structure of my frame, for a chamber-counsel, not for a pleader at the bar. But the call of Jesus Christ bids me cry aloud, and spare not. As His minister, I am debtor both to the Greek and the barbarian.[25] How can I be silent, when I have both ever before me, and my debt not paid? You would suggest that energies more restrained will eventually be more efficient. I am aware of this, and mean to act upon this principle in future, if the resolution is not formed too late. But you know how apt we are to outstep the bounds of prudence, when there is no kind monitor at hand to warn us of the consequences.

Had I been favoured with the one I wanted, I might not now have had occasion to mourn. You smile at my allusion, at least I hope so, for I am hardly in earnest. I have long since ceased to repine at the decree that keeps us as far asunder as the east is from the west, and yet am far from regretting that I ever knew you. The remembrance of you calls forth the exercise of delightful affections, and has kept me from many a snare. How wise and good is our God in all his dealings with his children! Had I yielded to the suggestion of flesh and blood, and remained in England, as I should have done, without the effectual working of his power, I should without doubt have sunk with my sisters into an early grave; whereas here, to say the least, I may live a few years, so as to accomplish a very important work. His keeping you from me appears also, at this season of bodily infirmity, to be occasion of thankfulness. Death, I think, would be a less welcome visitor to me, if he came to take me from a wife, and that wife were you. Now if I die, I die unnoticed, involving none in calamity. Oh that I could trust Him for all that is to come, and love Him with that perfect love, which casteth out fear; for to say the truth, my confidence is sometimes

---

25 Romans 1:14.

shaken. To appear before the Judge of quick and dead is a much more awful thought in sickness than in health. Yet I dare not doubt the all-sufficiency of Jesus Christ; nor can I, with the utmost ingenuity of unbelief, resist the reasonings of St. Paul, all whose reasons seem to be drawn on purpose to work into the mind the persuasion that God will glorify Himself by the salvation of sinners through Jesus Christ...

25th. --After another interval, I resume my pen. Through the mercy of God I am again quite well ... Yesterday I dined in a private way with _____. After one year's inspection of me, they [the English residents of Cawnpore] begin to lose their dread, and venture to invite me. Our conversation was occasionally religious, but topics of this nature are so new to fashionable people, and those upon which they have thought so much less than on any other, that, often from the shame of having nothing to say, they pass on to other subjects where they can be more at home. I was asked after dinner if I liked music. On my professing to be an admirer of harmony, cantos were performed and songs sung. After a time I inquired if they had no sacred music. It was now recollected, that they had some of Handel's, but it could not be found. A promise however was made, that next time I came, it should be produced. Instead of it, the 145th Psalm-tune was played, but none of the ladies could recollect enough of the tune to sing it. I observed, that all our talents and powers should be consecrated to the service of Him who gave them. To this no reply was made, but the reproof was felt. I asked the lady of the house if she read poetry, and then proceeded to mention Cowper, whose poems, it seems, were in the library; but the lady had never heard of the book.[26] This was produced, and I read some passages. Poor people! here a little, and there a little, is a rule to be observed in speaking to them.

---

26 William Cowper (1731-1800) was a friend of John Newton's and an established poet of both Christian and secular works.

26th. --From speaking to my men last night, and again to-day conversing long with some natives, my chest is again in pain, so much so that I can hardly speak. Well! now I am taught, and will take more care in future. My sheet being full, I must bid you adieu. The Lord ever bless and keep you. Believe me to be, with the truest affection,

Yours ever,

H. MARTYN.

Martyn's health continued to worsen. Though Rev. Daniel Corrie came to Cawnpore, lived with Martyn for a time, and helped him in his ministry, Martyn's health continued to sink. It seemed urgent that Henry leave the area and go elsewhere for his health. On Sept. 22, 1810, he wrote in his journal:

Was walking with L[ydia]; both much affected, and speaking on the things dearest to us both. I awoke, and behold, it was a dream! My mind remained very solemn and pensive; I shed tears. The clock struck three, and the moon was riding near her highest noon; all was silence and solemnity; and I thought with pain of the sixteen thousand miles between us. But good is the will of the Lord, even if I see her no more.[27]

Cawnpore, August 14, 1810.

With what delight do I sit down to begin a letter to my beloved Lydia! Yours of the fifth of February, which I received a few days ago, was written, I perceive, in considerable embarrassment. You thought it possible it might find me married, or about to be so.[28] Let me begin, therefore, with assuring you, with more truth than Gehazi[29] did his master, 'Thy servant went no whither;' my heart has not

---

27 *Life and Letters of Henry Martyn*, 272-273.

28 Daniel Corrie's sister had gone out to India, and some had tried to match her with Henry Martyn. Rumor in England had the two married, but there was never any such thought in Henry's mind.

29 The servant of the prophet Elisha (II Kings 4-5).

strayed from Marazion, or Gurlyn,[30] or wherever you are. Five long years have passed, and I am still faithful. Happy would it be if I could say that I have been equally true to my profession of love for Him who is fairer than ten thousand, and altogether lovely.[31] Yet, to the praise of his grace, let me recollect that twice five years have passed away since I began to know Him, and I am still not gone from Him. On the contrary, time and experience have endeared the Lord to me more and more; so that I feel less inclination, and see less reason for leaving Him. What is there, alas! in the world, even were it everlasting?

I rejoice at the accounts you give me of your continued good health and labours of love. Though you are not so usefully employed as you might be in India, yet as that must not be, I contemplate with delight, your exertions at the other end of the world. May you be instrumental in bringing many sons and daughters to glory. ...

We all live here in bungalows, or thatched houses, on a piece of ground enclosed. Next to mine is the church, not yet opened for public worship; but which we make use of at night with the men of the 53rd[32]. Corrie lives with me, and Miss Corrie with the Sherwoods. We usually rise at daybreak, and breakfast at six. Immediately after breakfast we pray together, after which I translate into Arabic with Sabat,[33] who lives in a small bungalow on my ground. We dine at twelve, and sit recreating ourselves with talking a little about dear friends in England. In

---

30   Places in Cornwall, where Lydia lived.

31   Song of Solomon 5:10, 16.

32   The 53rd or the Shropshire Regiment of Foot arrived in India in 1805, and in 1807 were stationed at Cawnpore. The regiment participated in the siege and capture of the fort of Adjighion in 1809, returning to Cawnpore in March 1810. *Historical Record of the Fifty-Third or The Shropshire Regiment of Foot.* London, 1849, xxvii – xxviii.

33   Sabat was an Arabian Moslem Henry Martyn had hired to help him with his translation work. Though he made a profession of conversion to Christianity, this was a sham. Sabat's pride, duplicity, and deceit caused Henry much difficulty.

the afternoon, I translate with Mirza Fitrut[34] into Hindostanee, and Corrie employs himself in teaching some native Christian boys whom he is educating with great care, in hopes of their being fit for the office of catechist. I have also a school on my premises for natives, but it is not well attended. There are not above sixteen Hindoo[35] boys in it at present; half of them read the book of Genesis. At sunset we ride or drive, and then meet at the church, where we often raise the song of praise, with as much joy, through the grace and presence of our Lord, as you do in England. At ten we are all asleep. Thus we go on. To the hardships of missionaries, we are strangers, yet not averse, I trust, to encounter them, when we are called. My work at present is evidently to translate; hereafter I may itinerate. Dear Corrie, I fear, never will,--he always suffers from moving about in the daytime. But I should have said something about my health, as I find my death reported at Cambridge. I thank God, I am perfectly well, though not very strong in my lungs; they do not seem affected yet, but I cannot speak long without uneasiness. From the nature of my complaint, if it deserves the name, it is evident that England is the last place I should go to. I should go home only to find a grave. How shall I therefore ever see you more on this side of eternity? Well! be it so, since such is the will of God: we shall meet, through grace, in the realms of bliss.

I am truly sorry to see my paper fail. Write as often as possible, every three months at least. Tell me where you go, and whom you see, and what you read.

17th. --I am sorry to conclude with saying, that my yesterday's boasted health proved a mistake; I was seized with violent sickness in the night, but to-day am better. Continue to pray for me, and believe me to be

Your ever affectionate,

H. MARTYN.

---

34 Mirza was a notable Hindostanee scholar from Benares.

35 'Hindoo' is an archaic spelling of 'Hindu'.

Henry had been working with Sabat on a Persian translation of the New Testament. When scholars in Calcutta read the manuscript, they thought it full of too many Arabic idioms and written in too scholarly a style to be suitable to most readers. Partly for his health and partly to improve his translation, Martyn decided to go into Arabia and Persia to consult with scholars there. He continued to write to Lydia along his journey:

From the Ganges, Oct. 6, 1810.

MY DEAREST LYDIA,

Though I have had no letter from you very lately, nor have anything particular to say, yet having been days on the water without a person to speak to, tired also with reading and thinking, I mean to indulge myself with a little of what is always agreeable to me, and sometimes good for me: for, as my affection for you has something sacred in it, being founded on, or at least cemented by, an union of spirit in the Lord Jesus, so my separation also from you, produces a deadness to the world, at least for a time, which leaves a solemn impression as often as I think of it. Add to this, that as I must not indulge the hope of ever seeing you again in this world, I cannot think of you without thinking also of that world where we shall meet. You mention in one of your letters my coming to England, as that which may eventually prove a duty. You ought to have added, that in case I do come, you will consider it a duty not to let me come away again without you. But I am not likely to put you to the trial. Useless as I am here, I often think I should be still more so at home. Though my voice fails me, I can translate and converse. At home I should be nothing without being able to lift up my voice on high. I have just left my station, Cawnpore, in order to be silent six months. I have no cough, nor any sign of consumption, except that reading prayers, or preaching, or a slight cold, brings on pain in the chest. I am advised, therefore, to recruit my strength by rest. So I am come forth, with my face towards Calcutta, with an ulterior view to the sea. ...

Farewell, beloved friend; pray for me, as you do I am sure, and doubt not of an unceasing interest in the heart and prayers of your ever affectionate,

H. MARTYN.

At sea, Coast of Malabar,[36] Feb. 4, 1811

The last letter I wrote to you, my dearest Lydia, was dated November, 1810. I continued in Calcutta to the end of the year, preaching once a week, and reading the Word in some happy little companies, with whom I enjoyed sweet communion, which all in this vale of tears have reason to be thankful for, but especially those whose lot is cast in a heathen land. On New Year's-day, at Mr. Brown's urgent request, I preached a sermon for the Bible Society, recommending an immediate attention to the state of the native Christians. At the time I left Calcutta they talked of forming an Auxiliary Society. Leaving Calcutta was so much like leaving England, that I went on board my boat without giving them notice, and so escaped the pain of bidding them farewell. In two days I met my ship at the mouth of the river, and we put to sea immediately. Our ship is commanded by a pupil of Swartz,[37] and manned by Arabians, Abyssinians, and others...

10th. --To-day my affections seem to have revived a little. I have been deceived in times past, and erroneously called animal spirits, joy in the Holy Ghost. Yet I trust that I can say with truth, 'To them who believe, He is precious' [I Pet. 2:7]. 'Yes, thou art precious to my soul,

---

36 Southwest of India.

37 Christian Friedrich Swartz, or Schwartz (1726-1798), along with Bartholomeus Ziegenbalg, was a German Lutheran missionary under Danish sponsorship who began a work among the Tamil people on the Madras coast of India. Schwartz extended the work to Tanjore, where he kept a school for half-caste children.

my transport and my trust.' No thought now is so sweet as that which those words suggest-- *'In Christ.'* Our destinies thus inseparably united with those of the Son of God, what is too great to be expected? 'All things are yours, for ye are Christ's!' [I Cor. 3:23]. We may ask what we will, and it shall be given to us. Now, why do I ever lose sight of Him, or fancy myself without Him, or try to do anything without Him? Break off a branch of a tree, and how long will it be before it withers? To-day, my beloved sister, I rejoice in you before the Lord, I rejoice in you as a member of the mystic body, I pray that your prayers for one who is unworthy of your remembrance may be heard, and bring down tenfold blessings on yourself. How good is the Lord in giving me grace to rejoice with His chosen, all over the earth; even with those who are at this moment going up with the voice of joy and praise to tread His courts and sing His praise! There is not an object about me but is depressing. Yet my heart expands with delight at the presence of a gracious God, and the assurance that my separation from His people is only temporary. On the 7th we landed at Goa, the capital of the Portuguese possessions in the East. I reckoned much on my visit to Goa; expecting, from its being the residence of the Archbishop and many ecclesiastics, that I should obtain such information about the Christians in India as would render it superfluous to make inquiries elsewhere, but I was much disappointed. Perhaps it was owing to our being accompanied by several officers, English and Portuguese, that the Archbishop and his principal agents would not be seen; but so it was, that I scarcely met with a man who could make himself intelligible. We were shown what strangers are usually shown, the churches and monasteries, but I wanted to contemplate man, the only thing on earth almost that possesses any interest for me. I beheld the stupendous magnificence of their noble churches without emotion, except to regret that the Gospel was not preached in them. In one of the monasteries we saw the tomb of Francis Xavier, the Apostle of India, most richly ornamented, as well as the room in which it stands, with paintings and figures in bronze, done in Italy. The Friar who showed us the tomb, happening to speak of the grace of God in the heart, without which, said he, as he held the sacramental wafer, the body of Christ profits nothing, I began a conversation with him, which, however, came to nothing...

18th. (Bombay)--Thus far I am brought in safety. On this day I complete my 30th year. 'Here I raise my Ebenezer; Hither by thy help I'm come.'[38] It is sweet to reflect that we shall at last reach our home. I am here amongst men who are indeed aliens to the commonwealth of Israel, and without God in the world.[39] I hear many of those amongst whom I live, bring idle objections against religion, such as I have answered a hundred times. How insensible are men of the world to all that God is doing! How unconscious of his purposes concerning his Church! How incapable, seemingly, of comprehending the existence of it! I feel the meaning of St. Paul's words-- 'Hath abounded toward us in all wisdom and prudence, having made known to us the mystery of his will, that he would gather in one all things in Christ' [Eph. 1:8-10]. Well! let us bless the Lord-- 'All thy children shall be taught of the Lord, and great shall be the peace of thy children.'[40] In a few days I expect to sail for the Gulf of Persia in one of the Company's sloops of war.[41]

Farewell, my beloved Lydia, and believe me to be, ever

Yours most affectionately,

H. MARTYN.

---

38 I Samuel 7:10-12. 'Ebenezer' means 'Stone of Help.'

39 Ephesians 2:12.

40 Isaiah 54:13.

41 The purpose of the war sloops in the Persian Gulf was to go against any Arab pirates operating in those waters.

Muscat, April 22, 1811

MY DEAREST LYDIA,

I am now in Arabia Felix. ...

We sailed from Bombay on Lady-day; and on the morning of Easter saw the land of Mehran in Persia. After another week's sail across the mouth of the Gulf, we arrived here, and expect to proceed up the Gulf to Bushire, as soon as we have taken in our water. You will be happy to learn that the murderous pirates against whom we were sent, having received notice of our approach, have all got out of the way; so that I am no longer liable to be shot in a battle, or decapitated after it, if it be lawful to judge from appearances. ... This last marine excursion has been the pleasantest I ever made, as I have been able to pursue my studies with less interruption than when ashore. My little congregation of forty or fifty Europeans does not try my strength on Sundays; and my two companions are men who read their Bible every day. In addition to all these comforts, I have to bless God for having kept me more than usually free from the sorrowful mind. ... I do not know anything more delightful than to meet with a Christian brother, where only strangers and foreigners were expected. This pleasure I enjoyed just before leaving Bombay; a ropemaker who had just come from England understood from my sermon that I was one he might speak to; so he came and opened his heart, and we rejoiced together. In this ship I find another of the household of faith. In another ship which accompanies us there are two Armenians who do nothing but read the Testament. One of them will, I hope, accompany me to Shiraz, in Persia, which is his native country.

We are likely to be detained here some days, but the ship that will carry our letters to India sails immediately, so that I can send but one letter to England, and one to Calcutta. When will our correspondence be established? I have been trying to effect it these six years, and it is only yet in train. Why there was no letter from you among those dated June and July, 1810, I cannot conjecture, except that you had not received any of mine, and would write no more. But I am not yet without hope that a letter in the beloved hand will yet overtake me somewhere. My kindest and most affectionate remembrances to all the Western circle. ... Read Eph. i. I cannot wish you all these spiritual blessings, since they are already yours; but I pray that we may have the spirit of wisdom and knowledge to know that they are ours. It is a chapter I keep in mind every day in prayer. We cannot believe too much or hope too much. Happy our eyes that they see, and our ears that they hear.

As it may be a year or more before I shall be back, you may direct one letter after receiving this, if it be not of a very old date, to Bombay; all after to Bengal, as usual. Believe me to be ever, my dearest Lydia,

Your most affectionate
H. MARTYN

Shiraz,[42] June 23, 1811

MY DEAREST LYDIA,

How continually I think of you, and indeed converse with you, it is impossible to say. But on the Lord's day in particular, I find you much in my thoughts, because it is on that day that I look abroad, and take a view of the universal church, of which I observe that the saints in England form the most conspicuous part. On that day too, I indulge myself with a view of the past, and look over again those happy days, when, in company with those I loved, I went up to the house of God with a voice of praise. How then

---

42 Shiraz, in modern Iran, was a center of Persian literary studies. Henry Martyn's overland journey from Brushire (modern Bander-e Bushahr) to Shiraz took nine days in intense heat, often over 120degrees. The heat caused Martyn to rapidly lose strength. His strength returned when he reached the coolness of the mountains and the valley of Shiraz.

shall I fail to remember her who, of all that are dear to me, is the dearest? It is true that I cannot look back upon many days, nor even many hours passed with you; --would they had been more!--but we have insensibly become acquainted with each other, so that, on my part at least, it may be said that separation has brought us nearer to one another. It was a momentary interview, but the love is lasting, everlasting. Whether we ever meet again or not, I am sure that you will continue to feel an interest in all that befalls me.

After the death of my dear sister, you bid me consider that I had one sister left while you remained; and you cannot imagine how consolatory to my mind this assurance is. To know that there is one who is willing to think of me, and has leisure to do so, is soothing to a degree which none can know but those who have, like me, lost all their relations.

I sent you a letter from Muscat in Arabia, which I hope you received; for if not, report will again erase my name from the catalogue of the living, as I sent no other to Europe. Let me here say, with praise to our ever gracious heavenly Father, that I am in perfect health; of my spirits I cannot say much; I fancy they would be better were 'the beloved Persis' by my side. This name, which I once gave you, occurs to me at this moment, I suppose because I am in Persia, intrenched [sic] in one of its valleys, separated from Indian friends by chains of mountains and a roaring sea, among a people depraved beyond all belief, in the power of a tyrant guilty of every species of atrocity.[43] Imagine a pale person seated on a Persian carpet, in a room without table or chair, with a pair of formidable mustachios, and habited as a Persian, and you see me.

26th. --Here I expect to remain six months. The reason is this: I found on my arrival here, that our attempts at

---

43   Fath Ali Shah (1797-1834), nephew of the founder of the Qajar dynasty which ruled Persia throughout the nineteenth century, was an autocrat of a decentralized regime.

Persian translation in India were good for nothing; at the same time they proposed, with my assistance, to make a new translation. It was an offer I could not refuse, as they speak the purest dialect of the Persian. My host is a man of rank,--his name Jaffier Ali Khan, who tries to make the period of my captivity as agreeable as possible. His wife, for he has but one, never appears; parties of young ladies come to see her, but though they stay days in the house, he dare not go into the room where they are. Without intending a compliment to your sex, I must say that the society here, from the exclusion of females, is as dull as it can well be. Perhaps, however, to a stranger like myself, the most social circles would be insipid. I am visited by all the great and learned; the former come out of respect to my country, the latter to my profession. The conversation with the latter is always upon religion, and it would be strange indeed, if with the armour of truth on the right hand and on the left, I were not able to combat with success, the upholders of such a system of absurdity and sin. As the Persians are a far more unprejudiced and inquisitive people than the Indians, and do not stand quite so much in awe of an Englishman as the timid natives of Hindostan, I hope they will learn something from me; the hope of this reconciles me to the necessity imposed on me of staying here; about the translation I dare not be sanguine. The prevailing opinion concerning me is, that I have repaired to Shiraz in order to become a Mussulman[44]. Others, more sagacious, say that I shall bring from India some more, under pretense of making them Mussulmans, but in reality to seize the place. They do not seem to have thought of my wish, to have them converted to my religion; they have been so long accustomed to remain without proselytes to their own. ...

---

44   'Mussulman' is archaic English for 'Muslim' or 'Moslem'.

July 2.--The Mohammedans[45] now come in such numbers to visit me, that I am obliged, for the sake of my translation-work, to decline seeing them. To-day one of the apostate sons of Israel was brought by a party of them, to prove the Divine mission of Mahomet[46] from the Hebrew Scriptures; but with all his sophistry he proved nothing. I can almost say with St. Paul, I feel continual pity in my heart for them, and love them for their fathers' sake, and find a pleasure in praying for them. While speaking of the return of the Jews to Jerusalem, I observed that the 'gospel of the kingdom must first be preached in all the world, and then shall the end come'[Matt. 24:14]. He replied with a sneer, 'And this event, I suppose you mean to say, is beginning to take place by your bringing the Gospel to Persia.'

5th.--I am so incessantly occupied with visitors and my work, that I have hardly a moment for myself. I have more and more reason to rejoice at my being sent here; there is such an extraordinary stir about religion throughout the city, that some good must come of it. I sometimes sigh for a little Christian communion, yet even from these Mohammedans I hear remarks that do me good; to-day, for instance, my assistant observed, 'How he loved those twelve persons?' 'Yes,' said I, 'and not those twelve only, but all those who shall believe in him;' as he said, 'I pray not for these alone, but for all them who shall believe on me through their word' [John 17:20]. Even the enemy is constrained to wonder at the love of Christ. Shall not the objects of it say, What manner of love is this?

… May we live near one another in the unity of the Spirit, having one Lord, one hope, one God and Father. In your prayers for me, pray that utterance may be given me, that I may open my mouth boldly, to make known the

---

45   'Mohammedan' is another term for a follower of Muhammad or a Muslim.

46   'Mahomet' is a variant of the name of the prophet 'Muhammad'.

mysteries of the Gospel. I often envy my Persian hearers the freedom and eloquence with which they speak to me. Were I but possessed of their powers, I sometimes think that I should win them all; but the work is God's, and the faith of his people does not stand in the wisdom of men, but in the power of God. Remember me as usual with the most unfeigned affection to all my dear friends. This is now the seventh letter I send you, without having received an answer.

Farewell, yours
Ever most affectionately,
H. MARTYN

Shiraz, Sept. 8, 1811

A courier on his way to the capital, affords me the unexpected pleasure of addressing my most beloved friend. It is now six months since I left India, and in all that time I have not heard from thence. The dear friends there, happy in each other's society, do not enough call to mind my forlorn condition. Here I am still, beset by caviling infidels, and making very little progress in my translation, and half disposed to give it up, and come away. My kind host, to relieve the tedium of being always within a walled town, pitched a tent for me in a garden a little distance, and there I live amidst clusters of grapes, by the side of a clear stream; but nothing compensates for the loss of the excellent of the earth [fellowship with Christians]. It is my business, however, as you will say, and ought to be my effort, to make saints, where I cannot find them. ...

I am happy to say that I am quite well, indeed never better; no returns of pain in the chest since I left India. May I soon receive the welcome news, that you also are well, and prospering even as your soul prospers. I read your letters incessantly, and try to find out something new, as I generally do, but I begin to look with pain at the distant date of the last. I cannot tell what to think, but I cast all my care upon

Him who hath already done wonders for me, and am sure that, come what will, it shall be good, it shall be best. How sweet the privilege, that we may lie as little children before Him! I find that my wisdom is folly, and my care useless, so that I try to live on from day to day, happy in His love and care. May that God who hath loved us, and given us everlasting consolation, and good hope through grace, bless, love, and keep my ever-dearest friend; and dwelling in the secret place of the Most High, and abiding under the shadow of the Almighty, may she enjoy that sweet tranquility [sic] which the world cannot disturb. Dearest Lydia! pray for me, and believe me to be, ever most faithfully and affectionately yours,

H. MARTYN

Shiraz, October 21, 1811.

... I think of you incessantly; too much, I fear, sometimes: yet the recollection of you is generally attended with an exercise of resignation to His will. In prayer I often feel what you described five years ago as having felt, --a particular pleasure in viewing you as with me before the Lord, and entreating our common Father to bless both His children. When I sit and muse, my spirit flies away to you, and attends you at Gurlyn, Penzance, Plymouth Dock, and sometimes with your brother in London. If you acknowledge a kindred feeling still, we are not separated, our spirits have met and blended. I still continue without intelligence from India; since last January I have heard nothing of any one person whom I love. My consolation is, that the Lord has you all under his care, and is carrying on His work in the world by your means; and that when I emerge, I shall find that some progress is made in India especially, the country I now regard as my own. Persia is, in many respects, a field ripe for the harvest. Vast numbers secretly hate and despise the superstition imposed on them, and as many of them as have heard the Gospel, approve it; but they dare not hazard their lives for the name of the Lord Jesus. I am sometimes asked whether the external appearance of Mohammedanism might not be retained with Christianity; and whether I could not baptize them without their believing in the divinity of Christ? I tell them, No. ...

Let the long, long period of darkness and sin at last give way to the brighter hours of light and liberty, which wait on the wings of the Sun of Righteousness. Perhaps we witness the dawn of the day of glory, and if not, the desire that we feel, that Jesus may be glorified, and the nations acknowledge His sway, is the earnest of the Spirit, that when He shall appear, we shall also appear with Him in glory. Kind love to all the saints who are waiting His coming.

Yours with true affection,
My ever dearest Lydia,
H. MARTYN.

During his months at Shiraz, Henry Martyn had many opportunities to present the gospel to Moslem intellectuals in the city. He also completed the Persian translation of the New Testament. He wanted to present the New Testament to the Persian king and left Shiraz at the end of May, 1812. The journey to Tebriz was a difficult one, and Martyn was in a high fever for two months. The king would not receive Martyn without a letter of introduction from the British ambassador. The English minister Sir Gore Ouseley did present the New Testament before the King, who expressed appreciation for it. The Ouseleys also tenderly cared for Martyn as he recovered in Tebriz from his feverish travels.

Tebriz, July 12, 1812.

MY DEAREST LYDIA,

I have only time to say that I have received your letter of February 14. Shall I pain your heart by adding, that I am in such a state of sickness and pain, that I can hardly write to you? Let me rather observe, to obviate the gloomy apprehension my letters to Mr. Grant[47] and Mr. Simeon may excite, that I am likely soon to be delivered from my fever. Whether I shall gain strength enough to go on, rests on our Heavenly Father, in whose hands are all my times. Oh, his precious grace! His eternal, unchanging love in Christ to my soul, never appeared more clear, more sweet, more strong. I ought to inform you that, in consequence of the state to which I am reduced by traveling so far overland, without having accomplished my journey, and the consequent impossibility of returning to India the same way, I have applied for leave to come on furlough to England. Perhaps you will be gratified by this intelligence; but oh, my dear Lydia, I must faithfully tell you, that the probability of my reaching England alive is but small; and this I say, that your expectations of seeing me again may be moderate, as mine are of seeing you. Why have you not written more about yourself? However, I am thankful for knowing that you are alive and well. I scarcely know how to desire you to direct. Perhaps Alexandria in Egypt will be the best place; another may be sent to Constantinople; for, though I shall not go there, I hope Mr. Morier will be kept informed of my movements. Kindest love to all the saints you usually mention.

Yours, ever most faithfully and affectionately,

H. Martyn.

On September 12, 1812 Henry Martyn left Tebriz for Constantinople, a 1300-mile journey which was only the first leg of his return trip to England. After 45 days, he succumbed to weakness and illness, never reaching Lydia in England or even Constantinople. The last words written in his diary were for October 6:

---

47 Charles Grant was one of the Directors of the East India Company who encouraged missionary activity in India and the appointment of evangelical chaplains.

No horses being to be had, I had an unexpected repose. I sat in the orchard, and thought, with sweet comfort and peace, of my God; in solitude my company, my friend and comforter. Oh, when shall time give place to eternity! When shall appear that new heaven and new earth wherein dwelleth righteousness! There, there shall in no wise enter in anything that defileth: none of that wickedness which has made men worse than wild beasts,--none of those corruptions which add still more to the miseries of mortality, shall be seen or heard of any more.[48]

He died and was buried by strangers and unbelievers at Tocat, Turkey, on October 16, 1812. He was 31. His genius was coupled with humility, and his love for the Lord was reflected in his passion for the Scriptures. Henry Martyn forsook all for Christ, and his life is his richest legacy.

Lydia died at the home of her sister on September 21, 1829. The two lovers at last were reunited and with their beloved Savior.

---

48   *Life and Letters of Henry Martyn*, 404.

In 1912, one hundred years after Henry Martyn's death, a centennial celebration of his life was held in Tocat, where a monument to his memory had been established. Though Martyn had died alone without a Christian present, one hundred years later, Christian missionaries and young Armenian pastors in Tocat honored his dedication to and sacrifice for his Lord. Just three years later, in 1915, most of these same pastors were killed in the Armenian genocide, pouring out their lives for their Christian faith as had Martyn.*

---

*For an account of the nineteenth-century missionary work in Tocat see *Against the Gates of Hell*, by Gordon and Diana Severance. University Press of America, 2003.

DIETRICH BONHOEFFER
AND
MARIA VON WEDEMEYER

(1906-1945)   (1924-1977)

'Our marriage ... must strengthen our resolve to do and
accomplish something on this earth.'
Dietrich Bonhoeffer

Dietrich Bonhoeffer was a German clergyman and theologian who had written much about the relationship between society and the church. After Hitler became dictator of Germany in 1933, Bonhoeffer joined the 'Confessing Church', the small group of Christians who called the church to defend the truths of the Christian faith against modern changes, especially those being fostered by the new Nazi government. Though the Confessing Church continued to proclaim its loyalty to the established government, Hitler's forces felt it a growing threat to their power and authority.

In April 1935, Bonhoeffer founded an 'underground', illegal seminary for the Confessing Church, which met at Finkenwalde. As the Nazi grip on Germany tightened, Bonhoeffer was forbidden to lecture at the University of Berlin, and in 1937 the Gestapo closed the Finkenwalde Seminary; twenty-seven students were imprisoned. The same year Dietrich himself published one of his most important books, *The Cost of Discipleship*, an explication of the costly discipleship required by Jesus' Sermon on the Mount.

Though he had contacts in America, which would have allowed him to teach and minister in the United States while Hitler expanded his rule in Germany and Europe, Dietrich returned to Germany in July 1939, after only a month at New York's Union Seminary. He didn't believe he would have any right to help the German church rebuild after the war unless he stayed with the church through its time of darkness. Soon after his return, Bonhoeffer began working with the Abwehr, the German intelligence department of the Armed Forces High Command. He became a double agent under Admiral Canaris, using his international church contacts to help in a coup d'état against Hitler. His work for the Abwehr kept Bonhoeffer from being drafted into the German fighting forces.

In 1941, Bonhoeffer was forbidden to print or publish. Soon after he became involved in 'Operation 7,' a rescue mission which smuggled fourteen Jews into Switzerland.

In the midst of his political activities, Bonhoeffer continued his theological work, though officially silenced by the government. He was writing his *Ethics*, which he hoped would be a guide for life in Germany and Europe after Hitler. In June 1942, Bonhoeffer was the guest of Ruth von Kleist-Retzow at Klein-Krössin, using her attic room for his writing. Mrs von Kleist-Retzow had been a friend and supporter of Bonhoeffer for some time and had been a prime financial backer of the independent seminary at Finkenwalde. That June, her granddaughter Maria was with her. Maria von Wedemeyer had just graduated from high school and was about to begin her national service year at the boarding school at Altenburg. The three had some wonderful conversations together. Dietrich and Maria walked in the garden - Maria had never met anyone who had been to America before.

Dietrich was highly affected by the 'delightful memory of those few, highly charged minutes,'[1] as he wrote to his friend Eberhard Bethge, but there was no way to arrange another meeting or write to Maria.

On August 22, Maria's father, Hans von Wedemeyer, was killed at Stalingrad. Maria came home, and soon after went to Berlin to care for her grandmother, who was recovering from an eye operation. Dietrich often visited Mrs von Kleist-Retzow when Maria was there, and the two had many occasions to talk. Maria later wrote:

> Dietrich's frequent visits surprised me, and I was impressed by his devotion. We often had long talks together at this time. It was a reunion under different circumstances than in June. Being still affected by my father's death, I needed Dietrich's help.

On October 26, Maria's brother Max, to whom she had been very close, was also killed in Russia. Maria went to the family home at Pätzig to be with her family. Grandmother sensed the attachment between Maria and Dietrich and invited Bonhoeffer to attend Max's memorial service, since he had confirmed him. Maria's mother, Ruth von Wedemeyer, became alarmed at this arrangement and wrote Bonhoeffer and asked him not to come.

When Maria learned what her mother had done, she sent Bonhoeffer a note saying that she had known nothing of her mother's letter and only learned of it through her grandmother. She thanked Dietrich for the letter he had sent her on her brother's death, for it did her much good. Dietrich quickly replied and thanked Maria for her clarification of the situation, writing he hoped to be able to stop by and see her soon.

Maria's mother was further alarmed by these developments and requested to Dietrich that they might meet together and discuss matters. She was concerned about the eighteen-year

---

1   Quoted in Dietrich Bonhoeffer and Maria von Wedemeyer (trans. John Brownjohn). *Love Letters from Cell 92,* London: Harper Collins Publishers, 1994, 284. All letters between Dietrich and Maria quoted in this collection are from this work, unless otherwise cited.

age difference between Dietrich and Maria and also about Bonhoeffer's resistance activities. She wanted Dietrich and Maria to have no contact or writing of letters for a year. Dietrich respected Mrs Wedemeyer's wishes, not wanting to take advantage of her during her time of grief over the death of her husband and son, yet his love for Maria continued unabated.

Though unable to see Dietrich, Maria's diary during the coming months was effervescent with joy, as she remained certain of Dietrich's love and affection. It seemed incredible to her that Dietrich would want to marry her, but she basked in the joy of that fact.

By the first of January, Maria told her mother that her decision to marry Bonhoeffer was firm. Maria's mother consented that Maria could write and tell Bonhoeffer of her decision, but she must continue to postpone any meeting or correspondence for another six months. Both looked upon the letters they exchanged in January as the date of their engagement.

[Pätzig] 13 January 1943

Dear Pastor Bonhoeffer,

I've known, ever since arriving home, that I must write to you, and I've looked forward to doing so.

I recently spoke with my mother and my uncle [Hans-Jürgen von Kleist-Retzow] from Kieckow. I'm now able to write to you, and to ask you to answer this letter.

I find it hard to have to tell you in writing what can scarcely be uttered in person. I would rather disown every word that demands to be said on the subject, because it makes things that were better conveyed quietly sound so crude and clumsy. But, knowing from experience how well you understand me, I'm now emboldened to write to you even though I've really no right whatever to answer a question which you have never asked me.

With all my happy heart, I can now say yes.

Please understand my mother's reluctance to waive the delay she imposed upon us. She still can't believe, from past experience, that our decision will hold good. And I myself am always saddened to think that Grandmother has told you only nice things about me, so you form a false picture of me. Perhaps I should tell you a lot of bad things about myself; because it makes me unhappy to think that you could love me for what I'm not.

But I can't believe that anyone can like me so much for what I really am. I certainly have no wish to hurt you, but I must say this anyway:

If you've realized that I'm not good enough, or that you no longer want to come to me, I beg you to say so. I can still ask you that now; and how infinitely harder it will be if I'm forced to recognize it later on. I myself am quite convinced that I need more time in which to put my decision to the test, and because I know my time in the Red Cross will be hard, it's essential to me.

This is *our* business alone, isn't it, not anyone else's. I'm so scared of what other people say, even Grandmother. Can you grant this request?

Thank you from the bottom of my heart for all you've done for me recently. I can only guess how difficult it must have been, because I myself have often found it hard to endure.

Yours, Maria

[Berlin] 17 January 1943, Sunday

Dear Maria,

Your letter took four days to get here - which it did only an hour ago! The next post leaves here in an hour's time, so it must bring you at least a preliminary greeting and word of thanks - even though the things I'd like to say haven't come to mind. May I simply tell you what is in my heart? I feel, and am overwhelmed by the realization, that I've been granted a gift beyond compare. I'd given up hope of it, after all the turmoil of recent weeks, and now the inconceivably great and happy moment has come, just like that, and my heart is opening wide and brimming over with gratitude and confusion and still can't take it in - the 'yes' that is to determine the entire future course of our lives. If we could speak together now, there would be so infinitely much to say - though all it would really amount to is a repetition of one and the same thing! Will we be able to see each other soon, without having once more to fear what other people say? Or is it still impossible for some reason? I think it *has* to be possible now.

And I can't speak otherwise than I've so often spoken in my heart in recent weeks - I want to call you what a man calls the girl with whom it is his desire and privilege to go through life, and who has given him her consent. Dear Maria, thank you for what you said, for all you have endured on my account, and for all you are to me and wish to be. Let us now be happy in each other. You must have whatever you need in the way of time and peace and quiet in which to test yourself, as you put it, just as you think fit. *With* your 'yes' I, too, can now wait patiently; without that yes I was finding it hard and would have found it increasingly so. Now that I know what you want and need, it's easy. I've no wish to coerce or alarm you in any way. I want to spare you and make the start of our life's happiness easy and joyful for you. I can well understand your wanting to be alone for a while. I've spent long enough alone in my time to know the blessings - but also the dangers - of solitude. I understand and have always understood in recent weeks - though not entirely without regret - that it cannot be easy for you to give me your consent, and I shall never forget that - and it's only this 'yes' of yours that can give me the courage to stop saying 'no' to myself. Don't say anything about the 'false picture' I may have of you. I don't want a 'picture', I want you; just as I beg you with all my heart to want me, not a picture of me - and you must surely know that those are two different things. ...

This letter must leave at once if you're to get it tomorrow. May God preserve you and both of us.

Your devoted Dietrich

I naturally won't say anything to your grandmother before you want me to. Anyway, I won't be seeing her in the immediate future. Why not write from Hanover[2] and tell her? My date of departure still isn't fixed, but I'm pretty sure it won't be long now. I shall then be away for about four weeks. I'm already looking forward very much to a letter from you.

Maria's grandmother had hinted to her of the dangers Bonhoeffer was in, and Maria began to worry. Thoroughly alarmed, she called Dietrich in Berlin. Her diary records her feelings, and Dietrich soon answered by letter as well:

Diary, 9 March 1943

I've spoken to you and heard your voice. Dietrich, dearest, can you still remember every word we exchanged? 'Hey,' you said, 'what's the matter?' And oh, how the tears rolled down my cheeks although I'd tried so hard not to cry and certainly hadn't done so since the lunch break. And at first you didn't understand what I was driving at. I put it so stupidly, didn't I? But then you laughed. It was so lovely, that laugh. To think you could laugh like that! I'm grateful to you for that most of all. When you laughed and told me not to worry, I knew all at once that it wasn't true, what Grandmother had said, and that all my worrying and weeping had been quite unnecessary, and that you were all right and glad that I'd

---

2   Maria was about to start work as a student nurse at the Clementinenhaus Hospital in Hanover.

called you. That was why you laughed, wasn't it, because you were glad. Afterwards I laughed too.

[Berlin] Tuesday night [9 March 1943]

Dear Maria,

My heart is still pounding audibly, and everything inside me has undergone a kind of transformation - from joy and surprise, but also from dismay that you were worried. I'm always doing silly things like this. If you were here and we could talk to each other I'd have told you what I stupidly told your grandmother. No, you needn't have a moment's worry - I'm not worried either. You do, of course, know from the little we've said to each other that danger exists not only there [on the battlefronts] but here at home as well, sometimes rather less so, sometimes rather more. What man of today has the right to shun it and shrink from it? And what woman of today should not share it, however gladly the man would relieve her of that burden? And how indescribably happy it makes the man if the woman he loves stands by him with courage, patience, and - above all - prayer. Dear, good Maria, I'm not being fanciful - something to which I'm far from prone - when I tell you that your presence-in-spirit has been a manifest help to me in recent weeks. That I should have caused you distress, however, genuinely saddens me a great deal. So now please be calm and confident and happy again, and think of me as you have hitherto and as I so constantly think of you. ...

I'm now off to Rome for several weeks. When will we be able to go there together?! ... And now may God protect you, dearest Maria - may he protect us both!

I love you very much and am thinking of you.

Yours, Dietrich

Bonhoeffer had planned to go to Rome for secret negotiations with the Vatican, but he was warned of the special dangers of the trip and did not go. On April 5, 1943, he was arrested in

Berlin and taken to the military prison of Tegel, a north-western suburb of Berlin. Maria learned of Dietrich's arrest while at Pätzig on April 18. Dietrich and Maria first met together after their engagement behind Tegel's prison walls. Of this first meeting Maria wrote in her diary:

> June 24, 1943 Our first meeting ... took place in the Reichskriegsgericht, and I found myself being used as a tool by the prosecutor, Roeder. I was brought into the room with practically no forewarning, and Dietrich was visibly shaken. He first reacted with silence, but then carried on a normal conversation; his emotions showed only in the pressure with which he held my hand.

> July 30. 1943 [On this day, Maria again visited. Her diary recorded the meeting:]
> ... I was sitting on the red plush sofa when you came in. Seeing you like that, I very nearly called you 'Sie'[3]. A well-fitting dark suit, a formal bow to the Oberstgerichtsrat[4] ... strangely unfamiliar.
> But when I looked into your eyes, I saw that dear, dark light in them, and when you kissed me, I knew I'd found you again - found you more completely than I'd ever possessed you before.
> It was all so different from the first time. You were calmer and more relaxed. But more confident, too. I sensed that most of all, and it was that which descended on my sad, dispirited heart and made me cheerful and happy. The things one talks about at such times! First names (the old topic), car-driving, the weather, the family. And yet it meant so much and outweighed the intervening month of loneliness. You caught hold of me at one point. Although I was inwardly so calm, I was shivering. It felt so good, your warm hand, that I wished

---

3   The polite, formal mode of 'you' in German.

4   Judge advocate of colonel's rank.

you would leave it there, although it transmitted a current that filled me up and left no room for thoughts. But you took it away. Don't you like being romantic?

Your eyes were with me. ...

On July 30 Dietrich was informed an indictment was being prepared against him, and he was responsible for his own lawyer. His writing privileges were extended, and he was allowed to write directly to Maria. The letters, however, were to be censored.

[Tegel] 30 July 1943

My dear Maria,

Isn't it wonderful that I can now write to you direct? How I've longed for this moment! I'm allowed to write every four days, so I'll alternate between you and my parents. Today has been so fraught with impressions, thought-provoking as well as heart-warming, that I've yet to recover composure completely, but I can't resist writing to you at once. How can I ever thank you for the love, loyalty and courage with which you're enduring everything, and with which you undertook another trip to the Reichskriegsgericht, which must surely be awful for you? It was so inexpressibly wonderful to be with you, even more so than the last time – and think how it will be when we're together with no one else around! I know I'm awfully bad at saying anything that will cheer and console you during these visits, and at showing how much I love you. I'm not cheerful and unselfish enough – it's the fault of this frightful prison, but you know all that, and if I talk too much about myself you must realize that you are always included in me. I'm never without you: the last few months have made me far more aware of that than I already was.

Your dear, dear letter has just arrived! So tomorrow you'll all be together on your father's birthday, and I shall think of you all. I was really very touched by what you wrote about your younger brothers and sisters and their remembering me [in their prayers]. Yes, I'll do my best to be a good older brother to them. At home I was almost the youngest, so I'm more delighted than I can say at the prospect of acquiring a horde of young brothers and sisters. May everything turn out as we hope and pray, and may I be able to bring you all something that will please you in return for what your family is giving me. Any depression I feel is always overcome by joyful anticipation of my first day at Pätzig.

I think it's splendid that you're tackling the violin, but you mustn't run down the guitar! It's a perfectly respectable instrument, not to be confused with the mandolin. We must go to a good guitar recital some time. In Mexico I spent an unforgettable summer's night listening to a great guitarist.

The bell has just rung for lights out. This letter will go off tomorrow morning. There's not much in it. My head is almost empty of thoughts today, but my heart is full of love - that's always there, even without many thoughts, and always with you. Goodbye, my dearest Maria. Go on being cheerful, patient, and brave, and don't forget me any more than I ever forget you, from dawn to dusk and in the night, when I wake. My cordial regards and thanks to your mother and grandmother, and a special word of greeting to each of your brothers and sisters.

I love and embrace you.

Yours, Dietrich

[Tegel] 12 August 1943

My dearest Maria,

... So now to your letter. You can't possibly imagine what it means to me, in my present predicament, to have you. I'm under God's special guidance here, I feel sure. To me, the way in which we found each other such a short time before my arrest seems a definite indication of that. Once again, things went *'hominum confusione et dei providentia.'*[5] It

---

5   'According to man's confusion and God's providence.'

amazes me anew every day how little I have deserved such happiness, just as it daily and deeply moves me that God should have put you through such an ordeal this past year, and that he so clearly meant me to bring you grief and sorrow, so soon after we got to know each other, to endow our love with the proper foundation and the proper strength. Moreover, when I consider the state of the world, the total obscurity enshrouding our personal destiny, and my present imprisonment, our union - if it wasn't frivolity, which it certainly wasn't - can only be a token of God's grace and goodness, which summon us to believe in him. We would have to be blind not to see that. When Jeremiah said, in his people's hour of direst need, that 'houses and fields [and vineyards] shall again be bought in this land,'[6] it was a token of confidence in the future. That requires faith, and may God grant us it daily. I don't mean the faith that flees the world, but the faith that endures *in* the world and loves and remains true to that world in spite of all the hardships it brings us. Our marriage must be a 'yes' to God's earth. It must strengthen our resolve to do and accomplish something on earth. I fear that Christians who venture to stand on earth on only one leg will stand in heaven on only one leg too.

I'm thoroughly in favor of your pastor marrying us, by the way. In these matters I think one should always do the most obvious thing. That's more important than any personal preference.

So now you've got the house full of people. How much I would have liked to see you running the household at this time! Your mother wrote me such a nice letter again, telling me all kinds of things. Please thank her very much indeed; I know what a sacrifice it must be for her to find the time to

---

6   Jeremiah 32:15.

write to me. But there's no greater pleasure in this place than getting letters from people. One rereads them innumerable times so as to share in their lives.

It's a cloudy, rainy day outside, a perfect accompaniment to my fruitless wait for the situation to resolve itself. But let us never forget how much we have to be thankful for, and how much good we experience even so; I have only to think of you, and all the little shadows of my soul disperse. So let us continue to be really patient for the rest of the time we're compelled to wait, and not waste a single hour grousing and grumbling. From God's standpoint, this time of waiting is immensely valuable; much depends on how we endure it and on whether we need not feel ashamed, later on, of having failed to recognize these months of testing as a gift from God. I'm convinced that our love and our marriage will derive eternal strength from this time of trial. So let us wait, with and for each other, until our wedding day dawns. It won't be much longer, my dear, dear Maria!

Please give my love to your mother and your brothers and sisters. ... Goodbye, dearest Maria, and may God preserve us and our families.

Your Dietrich, who looks forward from one letter to the next, embraces you!

Pätzig, 23 August 1943

My beloved you!

Will you be writing me today? I seem to see you as vividly as if I were sitting beside you. Your whole surroundings, your gestures, your hands and eyes. You'll write me the nicest letter - and - whatever it's like - it will bring me a sunny day. No, not just a day. It will bring me a piece of the sun's gold, one that I can absorb deep inside - one that outlasts any rain or storm and warms every little part of me with its radiant light. Thank you now and always, just for wanting to write to me.

You knew, of course, that yesterday was the anniversary of Father's death. He was wounded at three in the morning and died at six. I went for a walk in the woods at that time, which was good. Do you, too, think it's wrong to ask for a 'why?' Surely it's only wrong if you ask reproachfully, without genuinely requesting an answer. I believe there's an answer to every 'why,' even here on earth. It's just that we can't sense it and are unable to grasp it for that reason. But isn't the answer really inside us, as long as we don't keep asking for more? Please don't tell me, like the others, that I've got a romantic streak, but I know for sure that Father still exists - not in the form of a fading memory, but abidingly and still quite perceptibly. If it weren't so, this period of mourning would have been very different for us all. I believe that Father is very fond of you - he always understood me better than all the rest.

You see, now you've come to me, and I love you very much and want nothing more than to be a good helpmate and make you happy. I don't know how I'll manage it, and I only dare to hope that I'll do so because you believe I can. But please help me.

Thank you for being what you are to me.

Yours, Maria

[Tegel] 9 September 1943

My dearest Maria.

... I'm so glad you're not in Berlin now. It makes the air-raid nights easier, and your 34-strong household must be giving you plenty to do. Besides, it's very reassuring to know you're busy with your trousseau. I picture that in every detail and in full colour, and I'm glad of it; it's such an image of calm, confidence, and happiness. When shall I see and admire and delight in all those things? And when shall we use them together in our daily life and, at the same time, recall the strange times in which they originated? It can't be very much longer. But we'll be patient to the last and look upon this difficult time of waiting, too, as God's way with us, until one day, perhaps, we gain a better understanding of why it was good for us. My dearest Maria, you can't know what it means to me to be at one with you in this. How strange your path through life must often seem to you these days. But one has to climb a mountain, too, in zigzags, or one would never reach the top, and from up there one can often see quite clearly why such a route was necessary. Some time read Gottfried Arnold's hymn, a very special favorite of mine, though few people know it. The text and tune are difficult, almost too difficult for a congregational hymn, but it grows on one. It begins, 'So führst Du doch ...' and it's in the hymn book.[7]

Just imagine, your letter of 23 August, the day after the anniversary of Father's death, has just arrived. You don't expect me to answer it, do you? I can't, not on paper. I can only thank you for writing to me and writing the way you did. It really is high time we saw and spoke to each other alone, and walked together through the woods at Pätzig!

My fond love to your mother, also to your brothers and sisters. Goodbye for now, my dear Maria. You're with me throughout the day from morning to night. God preserve you and all of us.

With all my heart.

Yours, Dietrich

[Tegel] 20 September 1943

Dearest Maria,

Autumn begins tomorrow. These last few weeks, whenever people have spoken of autumn coming early, I've disliked the sound of the word. The changing seasons are harder on one in here than outside. You'll now be spending a lot of time in the forest hides at dusk and before daybreak. I'm so

---

7   Arnold's hymn in the *Evangelical Hymnal for Brandenburg and Pomerania*, 1931, 230 begins 'Right gladly, Lord, thou leadest thus Thy people.'

fond of those autumn mornings when the sun breaks slowly through the mist, but I know that, wherever you are, you'll be waiting with me every day and every hour. This is turning into a wait whose outward purpose I fail to understand, and whose inward purpose has to be rediscovered daily. The last few months have deprived us both of a great deal. Time is today's most precious commodity, for who can tell how much more of it a person has been granted? Yet I refuse to believe that our past and present separation is time lost, either for each of us individually or for both together. We have grown together in a way that differs from our expectations and desires, but there are, and will doubtless continue to be, other times when all will ultimately depend on our being of one mind and sticking together. Your life would have been very different - easier, simpler, more predictable - had our paths not crossed a year ago, but I'm only troubled by that thought for brief moments at a time. I believe that you, as well as I, had reached a stage in life at which our meeting was inevitable. Neither of us had any fundamental desire for an easy life, much as we can both take pleasure in life's lovely, happy times, and much as we doubtless yearn for such times today. For both of us, I believe, happiness lies elsewhere, in a more remote place that not only passes many people's understanding, but will continue to do so. At bottom, we both seek tasks to perform. Each of us has hitherto sought them separately, but from now on they'll be common tasks in which we shall fully grow together - if God grants us the requisite time. ...

Goodbye for now, my dearest Maria, and wait a little longer! It's good to know you're waiting with me! My love to your mother and your brothers and sisters. It won't be long before I can be with you - it can't be much longer! Till then, patience and courage! With all my heart,

Yours, Dietrich

Dietrich also made his will on September 20; the next day he was given his indictment. Though not charged with high treason or treasonable activity, he was charged with undermining the morale of the armed forces. The long waiting would continue.

Pätzig, 29 September 1943

My dearly beloved Dietrich,

... Don't get tired and depressed, my dearest Dietrich, it won't be much longer now. It can't be much longer, and then we'll be together. It'll be lovelier than we can now imagine in our wildest dreams, and we'll be happier than we've ever been before.

Yes, I often read Gottfr. Arnold's hymn, and am grateful for it. I also read the 103rd Psalm and tell myself that we'll be hearing it together before long. You must look forward to that with me, very, very much. You mustn't get depressed when you think of me. You must be happy and know that I'm happy too, Dietrich, every time I think of you. Happy that I have you at this time, that I can sense your nearness, that I'm privileged to love you and can help you a little by doing so. Let us both honour God 'with ever joyful hearts' and never forget the good he has done us,

Always and only your Maria

[Tegel] 30 September 1943

... Dearest Maria, in all our daily hopes and prayers for a speedy reunion, let us never forget to thank God for all he has given us and continues to give us every day. Then all our thoughts and plans will become clearer and calmer, and we shall readily and willingly accept our personal destiny. This week's Gospel [Luke 17:11-17] - about gratitude - is one of those which I love and treasure most.

Maria visited Dietrich October 7.

Pätzig, 8 October 1943

My very dear, beloved Dietrich,

Three letters and one visitor's permit, all at once, are a bit too much for a brimming heart like mine. How can

I tell you about it in a silly, ridiculous letter? When a letter comes from you and I read it, it's as if you're sitting beside me and speaking to me in a way we've never spoken yet, but as we shall speak when we're alone together. When you speak to me that way, all I want to do is listen. It's like music, not just words. In words one so easily talks at cross purposes, but in music one experiences a communion. ...

You say my life would have been simpler and easier if I'd never met you. Dietrich, I don't regret a single hour since I've known you, nor a single thought, nor the tears and happy laughter. Shall I tell you something else? Shall I tell you that I was utterly desperate when I lost the two people dearest to me, that I felt empty and lonely and crushed by the love I felt within me but could no longer give. No, Dietrich, my life wouldn't have become simple, but meaningless and shallow. And then you came along, and I realized you were coming to me; and you'll be my father and brother and more than everyone else put together - indeed, you are that already. Please don't write that again. I already belong to you so completely, I don't want even to entertain such an idea. ...

I do so hope this letter reaches you soon and gives you some idea of how close to you I am. I send you all my love and keep you always in my heart.

Yours, Maria

Maria visited Dietrich November 10.

[Tegel] 10 November 1943

My dear, dear Maria,

I must at least attempt to write the letter I'm not really entitled to write you for another three days. I shall then have to wait seven days for the coveted afternoon when I can converse with you not only in my thoughts but on paper, but still! It was so good, your being here today. I hadn't dared to hope that you would come, after what you wrote about

Ruth-Alice's[8] state of health, but you came anyway. It was far too short - I naturally spent yesterday and today noting down all the questions and requests I had for you, so as not to forget them, and I just as naturally forgot them all. But that was quite unimportant compared to the simple fact that you sat beside me on the sofa for a while and were with me. You'd been up all night, caught a train, and come here straight from the station - probably without any lunch - and all you said was, 'It's only natural!' Yes, Maria, but the very fact that it *is* natural - that's the miracle, the good fortune that forever passes my understanding, the utterly *un*natural thing! Your picture, with which I have to be content for weeks on end, is hanging in front of me, but now I hear your voice once more. And your laugh - even when we laugh we're a trifle sad, aren't we? I see your eyes, I feel your hand. Everything is absolutely real again. How can I thank you for everything? I can't, I can only tell you that all is well when you're with me. And now let us help one another to endure the remainder of this hard trial of patience in the proper way, thankfully and calmly. Is it wrong to hope that, after the strain of the last few months, the happiness that awaits us will be all the more glorious - indeed, that we have already borne a part of the cross that burdens every marriage? I cannot tell, we mustn't anticipate God's ways, but we do at least know that he never abandons us, even in hard times, but binds us together still more firmly - and nothing else matters. ...

Goodbye for now, dearest Maria. May God preserve us till we're together in freedom. Give my special regards to your mother, also to your brothers and sisters and your grandmother. But to you, above all, goes my heartfelt love.

Yours, Dietrich

---

8   Ruth-Alice von Bismarck was Maria's sister; she had had a little boy at the end of September and was ill for some time after that. Maria's mother went to stay with her, and Maria was left in charge of Pätzig for a time, after which Maria went to care for her sister.

The heavy bombing of Berlin in November, 1943 damaged Tegel Prison. Nearly all the windows were shattered. The Reichskriegsgericht was also damaged, and fire destroyed all the papers essential for Bonhoeffer's trial. Officials were called in to reconstruct the material. Pätzig itself was full of refugees from the Berlin air raids.

[Tegel] 1 December 1943

My dearest Maria,

... Your Advent wreath, which I've hung on the wall around the little Nativity picture, and the warm coat, which keeps the cold at bay together with Max's scarf, remind me of you constantly and fill me time and again with gratitude for all you think, feel, and do for my sake. It's so genuinely peaceful, quiet, and Advent-like here in my cell, and the countless Advent and Christmas carols I've known since childhood surround me like so many benevolent spirits. So you've really no need to worry about me, just as I know that you're safely rehearsing your Nativity play and looking after your air-raid refugees. We both know what we're missing and suffering, but it's better to think of each other calmly and confidently than fretfully and anxiously.

I think we're going to have an exceptionally good Christmas. The very fact that every outward circumstance precludes our making provision for it will show whether we can be content with what is truly essential. I used to be very fond of thinking up and buying presents, but now that we have nothing to give, the gift God gave us in the birth of Christ will seem all the more glorious; the emptier our hands, the better we understand what Luther meant by his dying words: 'We're beggars, it's true.' The poorer our quarters, the more clearly we perceive that our hearts should be Christ's home on earth. So let us approach this Christmas-tide not only undaunted but with complete confidence. And should God's mercy reunite us this season, we shall have the finest earthly Christmas gifts in each other! How wonderful it would be for our families, too! You wouldn't believe how much I miss every one of them. I positively hunger for people after so many months of solitude. However, I'm afraid I won't at first be equal to the company of many people for any length of time - even in the old days I could only endure family gatherings, of which I'm very fond in themselves, by periodically taking refuge in my room for half an hour. This time, I hope you'll take refuge there with me! ...

Time to close again. It's always like a little farewell when another letter ends. But soon we won't be forever saying goodbye, but celebrating a really long, long reunion! Goodbye for now, dearest Maria. Give my love to your mother, grandmother, and brothers and sisters, and take a kiss from

Your Dietrich

Maria visited Dietrich December 10.

[Berlin] 10 December 1943

My Dietrich, my all,

Here I am again, sitting down to write and thank you with a sheet of paper in front of me, and I have a so much stronger and more immediate sense of your nearness than words and letters can ever, in their roundabout way, express. A few hours ago we were sitting side by side. I see you so vividly before me and recall so much of what you said. I'm filled with great happiness and amazement, because that happiness remains forever unfathomable - in fact I can't quite believe in it. All that grieves me at other times disappears when I'm sitting beside you and can look at you, and all that remains is a great big wonderful 'You'! Saying goodbye to you had never seemed harder and the door never as pitiless, but you mustn't look sad - you must tell yourself that I'm at your side, that my heart goes with you, and that, if I weren't fully committed to you, I should be empty and insubstantial. Everything else remains a dream, and even in that dream there's nothing I could possibly see or hear without thinking of you. You've robbed me of my thoughts, and I've no wish to own them any longer - they all belong to you. I hardly slept, thanks to your book.[9] I love it, though I didn't read a word of it. It merely lay beside me, and I was happy to have it there. Something from you for me! And I can't help reading your inscription again and again and feeling glad of it. I'm so grateful to you for loving me.

And now Christmas is coming and you won't be there. We shall sing 'Friede auf Erden' [Peace on earth] and pray together, but we shall sing 'Ehre sei Gott in der Höhe!' [Glory be to God on high] even louder. That is what I pray for you and me and all of us, that the Saviour may throw open the gates of heaven for us at darkest night on Christmas Eve, so that we can be joyful in spite of everything.

I love and kiss you.

Yours, Maria

Dietrich's trial had been scheduled for December 17, and there was some hope he would be released by Christmas, but the trial was postponed.

[Tegel] 13 December 1943

My dearest Maria,

Without abandoning all hope that things may yet take a turn for the better just in time, I must now write you a Christmas letter. Be brave for my sake, dearest Maria, even if this letter is your only token of my love this Christmas-tide. We shall both

---

9   During her visit, Bonhoeffer had given her an inscribed copy of an anthology of love letters, *Briefe der Liebe aus 8 Jahrjunderten [Love Letters from Eight Hundred Years]*, edited by Friedrich Percyval Reck-Malleczewen.

experience a few dark hours - why should we disguise this from each other? We shall ponder the incomprehensibility of our lot and be assailed by the question of why, over and above the darkness already enshrouding humanity, we should be subjected to the bitter anguish of a separation whose purpose we fail to understand. How hard it is, inwardly to accept what defies our understanding; how great is the temptation to feel ourselves at the mercy of blind chance; how sinister the way in which mistrust and resentment steal into our hearts at such times; and how readily we fall prey to the childish notion that the course of our lives reposes in human hands! And then, just when everything is bearing down on us to such an extent that we can scarcely withstand it, the Christmas message comes to tell us that all our ideas are wrong, and that what we take to be evil and dark is really good and light because it comes from God. Our eyes are at fault, that is all. God is in the manger, wealth in poverty, light in darkness, succour in abandonment. No evil can befall us; whatever men may do to us, they cannot but serve the God who is secretly revealed as love and rules the world and our lives. We must learn to say: 'I know how to be abased, and I know how to abound: in any and all circumstances I have learned the secret of facing plenty and hunger, abundance and want. I can do all things in him who strengthens me' (Phil. 4:12-13) - and this Christmas, in particular, can help us to do so. What is meant here is not stoical resistance to all extraneous occurrences, but true endurance and true rejoicing in the knowledge that Christ is with us.

Dearest Maria, let us celebrate Christmas in that way. Be as happy with the others as a person can only be at Christmas-time. Don't entertain any awful imaginings of me in my cell, but remember that Christ, too, frequents prisons, and that he will not pass me by. Besides, I hope to find myself a good book for Christmas and read it in peace.

May you do likewise. A little oblivion is permissible in view of everything else. ... Dearest Maria, let's not talk of what we both feel; we know it, and every word merely makes the heart heavier. Above all, let us be careful not to feel sorry for ourselves; to do so would truly be a blasphemy on God, who means us well. ... my beloved Maria, be greeted, embraced and kissed by

Your Dietrich

Maria visited Dietrich December 22 and brought him bundles of Christmas presents. Maria later recalled this occasion:

The fact that I brought a sizable Christmas tree all the way from home created great hilarity with both the guards and Dietrich. He remarked that maybe if he moved his cot out of his cell and stood up for the Christmas season he could accommodate the tree comfortably. It ended up in the guards' room where Bonhoeffer was invited to enjoy it. He teased me about it often and complained that I had not brought an Easter bunny for Easter. But he also wrote: 'Isn't it so that even when we are laughing, we are a bit sad?'

[Tegel] Christmas Eve, 1943

My beloved Maria,

This is a time when there's so much to say that silence is the only real answer. One's heart is so full of good, peaceful, grateful thoughts and knows that it's so safe from all dangers and tribulations that it would like to share some of what it has undeservedly been given. I have just read the Christmas story, looked at the Nativity pictures in your lovely book, and said a few hymns to myself. And, while doing all those things, I've thought of you and yours, of my brethren in the field, of the people in this building. In front of me, lit by your candles, stands the little Madonna you gave me, the present from your father. Behind it are the open texts with the 'praying hands' on their left and, on their right, your photos lying open in the case you made for me. Just above them hangs your Advent wreath, and behind me on the edge of the bed I've laid out the gloves you made for me, the books you chose for me, also the ones from Mother and Grandmother, and the gingerbread. On my wrist is the watch Father was wearing when he died, which you gave me, brought me, and strapped on my wrist yourself. You're all around me, Maria mine - I see you in my cell wherever I look. You're far away, it's true; you'll probably be in church at this hour - it's 5 p.m. - and you'll be thinking of me and praying to God for me, as you do every day. It's so hard to be apart when one is in love, but we're never really apart, are we? Never, never. How shall I ever be able to compensate you for all the distress I've caused you - truly without meaning to - in recent months? Only, dearest Maria, by loving you for as long as I live and, over and above that, by asking for your love, which cannot but seem miraculous to me. ...

Please convey my heartfelt thanks to Mother and Grandmother for their messages. What an abundance of human love we're privileged to feel assured of, and how many invisible messages, good wishes and prayers I receive when I think of all members of our numerous families. It's also my privilege to know that, this evening, many of my former students will be thinking of me on the various battlefronts. As for those who have been killed - over thirty of them - and are celebrating an eternal Christmas with God, they are united with us and the whole of Christ's Church in a way that transcends our perception and understanding.

My eyes have just lighted on your parcel again. How festively you wrapped it for me. It was a big surprise to receive it at noon today. I still haven't thanked you for the cotton sweater, which can only have been knitted by you. I was so delighted with it, I put it on right away. It's wonderfully warm and light at the same time.

My dearest Maria, steadfastly believing in God's love, which summons us to Jesus Christ, and in our love for each other, and sustained by the love of our many relatives and friends, let us enter on the New Year with confidence and good cheer.

Ever yours Dietrich

The letters, the waiting, and the monthly visitor's permits continued. Bonhoeffer no longer expected to be released, but expected to be sent to a concentration camp. His trial continued to be postponed. Maria took a job as a governess for her cousin Hedwig von Truchsess at Bundorf in Lower Franconia.

Bundorf, 7 March 1944

My dearest Dietrich,

Everyone is talking about that big daylight raid on Berlin. It must have been awful. I've only one recourse, and that's to take my troubles and fears and seek refuge with you. You write that one's worries should always become prayers. Thank you for telling me that. You're so good at resolving my big inner problems with a simple word or two. I first sensed that at the Schleichers' musical evening, and I've often been thankful for it since. ...

When we're together later on, we'll be grateful to God for giving us this time. God must love you very dearly if he visited this on you; he has deprived you of a great deal in order to give you a great deal more. And he loves me too, because he granted me the privilege of becoming engaged to you a year ago - and he couldn't have done so at a better stage, could he? Imagine if we'd had to live through this period not only apart but spiritually alone. And can there be anything finer for a woman than to be close to her man and able to help him a little? Our tasks here on earth are only accomplished by the amount of love we can bring to them. I shall always be grateful for every scrap of love bestowed on me, and I'll pass it all on to you, my dearest Dietrich. ...

I must tell you something really awful: theology strikes me as an incomprehensible discipline. Whenever I've come across it - our conversations have never been that theological, I'm happy to say - I always get the feeling that it's seeking an intellectual explanation for what is quite simply a question of faith. And if one first has to grasp an article of faith with the intellect, one just doesn't believe it any longer.

I recognize the need to interpret the Word. However, I once attended three days of Bible study at Altenburg, and on all three days we listened to lectures on the Resurrection followed by lively debates during which every conceivable view and opinion was aired. Having endured those days with polite sighs, I came to the following conclusion:

Either you believe in the Resurrection or you don't, but if two people can wrangle over minutiae for so long without reaching agreement, there's no better proof that neither of them believes in it! ... Now, when I pick up a theological book, I construe it as an interpretation of the Word that rejects all uncertainty as to whether it's correct or incorrect. I simply find these matters too sacred to play off one opinion against another.

'Pooh,' you'll say, 'how stupid she is!' (Perhaps I'm only writing this to convince you of the fact.) But please, tell me some time where I'm going wrong and why a pastor always has to be a theologian as well. ...

The next time I'm with you we'll forget in a flash what a terribly long time I've had to spend down here, and we'll simply be happy to be together. Meantime, keep well and be as patient as you have been up to now. Let's always be together in spirit, and be kissed by

Your Maria

[Tegel] 16 April 1944

Dearest Maria,

Although one birthday letter is already on its way to you, I can't resist writing to you again - in fact I'd like to write you a birthday letter every day. You're twenty years old! I'm thoroughly ashamed to recall how ignorant I was at that age, and how replete your own life already is, by comparison, with experiences and tasks of the utmost importance. I still believed then that life consisted of ideas and books, and wrote my first book, and was, I'm afraid to say, inordinately proud of it. But what did I give anyone at that stage? Whom did I help? Whom did I make glad and happy? What did I really know of the things I wrote about? And you? You don't write books, fortunately; you do, know, learn, and fill with real life that which I have only dreamed of. Perception, volition, action, emotion, and suffering don't disintegrate in your case; they're a grand totality of which one constituent reinforces and complements the other. You yourself don't realize that, and it's much the best that way, and perhaps I shouldn't mention it at all - so forget it and always remain as you are. Remain so for my sake, because that's what I need, what I've found in you, and what I love - the whole, undivided object of my longing and desire. ... I'm sometimes overwhelmed by the thought of how hard I'm making things for you - forgive me, you truly deserve better, infinitely better - but then I take courage from your letters and your presence, and I marvel and marvel at the unadulterated joy, love, patience, and strength I find in you. I can't understand it, but I can believe it and cling to it and be happy and glad of it, through and through, my beloved Maria! You don't want me to reproach myself on your account, but simply to love you, and that's what I want too, nothing else: to love you so much that you can feel none of the pain I'm compelled to inflict on you.

If only I could tell you that on your birthday, all alone with you, but I still have to write it - and for how much longer? Yesterday I left this building for the first time in months. They were very polite, but told me that I would have to be patient for quite a while longer; there was no prospect of any new development before Whitsun. I'm afraid the early summer months will be over before the longed-for day arrives. Dearest Maria, I wanted to write and tell you this at once, because it naturally troubles me a great deal and I don't want you to hear it from anyone else. It's hard to understand why it must be so, and it clothes our future in an uncertainty that can only be surmounted by our mutual love, our fidelity and patience, and our submission to the will and guidance of God. I should have said 'trust,' not 'submission,' but it's probably no accident that I penned the latter word first, and the road from submission to trust is ever new and ever difficult. ...

Might it please you a little to have the Spanish lamp on the bookshelf in my room? I've always liked it, and it has been my constant companion for fifteen years. I should be happy to know that it's in your room and find it there [when I come]. It also gives a pretty light. Please let me give it to you for your birthday. Although it's far from being what I'd like to give you, it's a part of my life and couldn't have a better home than with you. Goodbye for now, my dear, beloved Maria. May God grant us a happy day, a happy reunion, and, above all, a happy heart!

Be tenderly embraced and kissed and loved by

Your Dietrich

Maria was becoming increasingly alarmed by Dietrich's imprisonment as the chances of the two being reunited seemed to dwindle. She began to suffer from fainting fits during this emotional crisis, but her love for Dietrich and their engagement remained strong. Maria and Dietrich both knew they were somehow part of God's plan and trusted Him through the days of strain and separation.

On July 20, 1944, an attempt was made on Hitler's life, but the coup failed. A detailed investigation was organized and military legal authorities were stripped of their power. SS authorities took control of Tegel Prison.

[Tegel] 13 August 1944

My dearest Maria,

It always takes so long these days for our letters to reach their destination. It's probably the fault of the air raids to which the south of Germany, in particular, has so often been subjected in recent weeks. I've received only one letter from you in almost six weeks, and I'm afraid my parents' news of you was similar the last time they visited me. But you know, letters are such a feeble token of our belonging to each other that our thoughts and prayers are bound to express it best of all. And that they do, whether or not letters arrive, don't they? So now you've started work in Berlin. Hard work has for centuries been extolled as the finest remedy for troubles and cares. Many people consider the most beneficial aspect of work to be its tendency to numb the psyche. Personally, I think what really matters is that the right kind of work renders one unselfish, and that a person whose heart is filled with personal interests and concerns develops a desire for such unselfishness in the service of others. So I hope from the bottom of my heart that your new job grants you that boon, and that the greater its difficulties, the greater will be your sense of spiritual liberation. ... I've recently, and with great enjoyment, reread the memoirs of Gabriele von Bülow-Humboldt. She was separated from her fiancé for three whole years, shortly after her engagement! What immense patience and forbearance people had in those days, and what great 'tensile strength'! Every letter was over six weeks in transit. They learned to do what technology has deprived us of, namely, to commend each other daily to God and put their trust in him. We are now relearning that, and we should be thankful, however hard it is.

My beloved Maria, let us never lose faith in what befalls us; all of it is bestowed on us by good, kindly hands. I shall be thinking of you a great deal on the 22nd. Father is with God. He is only a step or two ahead of us. Let us think of him and Max with joy in our hearts and pray that Mother continues to find the consolation that has been hers throughout the past two years. Goodbye for now, beloved Maria, and may God preserve us all.

With all my faithful heart,
Dietrich

At the end of August, Maria left Bundorf and went to Berlin to live with the Bonhoeffers. She helped Dietrich's parents and was able to care for him more at the Tegel prison. This was a time of increasing investigation and arrests. On September 22, the Gestapo discovered Admiral Canaris' diaries, which detailed the resistance against Hitler. Bonhoeffer had worked out an escape plan with his guard, but abandoned it when he learned his brother Klaus and brother-in-law Schleicher had also been arrested.

On October 8, 1944, the Gestapo took Bonhoeffer from Tegel Prison to the underground cells at State Security Headquarters in Prinz-Albert Strasse. The evidence now against him was so clear that there was no hope for release apart from a liberation from the Allies. Conditions were much harsher at the SS headquarters. Maria was not allowed to see Bonhoeffer, and he was allowed to write only three Christmas letters; one was to Maria.

[Prinz-Albrecht-Strasse] 19 December 1944
My dearest Maria,

I'm so glad to be able to write you a Christmas letter, and to be able, through you, to convey my love to my parents and my brothers and sisters, and to thank you all. Our homes will be very quiet at this time. But I have often found that the quieter my surroundings, the more vividly I sense my connection with you all. It's as if, in solitude, the soul develops organs of which we're hardly aware in everyday life. So I haven't for an instant felt lonely and forlorn. You yourself, my parents - all of you including my friends and students on active service - are my constant companions. Your prayers and kind thoughts, passages from the Bible, long-forgotten conversations, pieces of music, books - all are invested with life and reality as never before. I live in a great, unseen realm of whose real existence I'm in no doubt. The old children's song about the angels says 'two to cover me, two to wake me,' and today we grown-ups are no less in need than children of preservation, night and morning, by kindly, unseen powers. So you mustn't think I'm unhappy. Anyway, what do happiness and unhappiness mean? They depend so little on circumstances and so much more on what goes on inside us. I'm thankful every day to have you - you and all of you - and that makes me happy and cheerful.

Superficially, there's little difference between here and Tegel. The daily routine is the same, the midday meal is considerably better, breakfast and supper are somewhat more meagre. Thank you for all the things you've brought me. I'm being treated well and by the book. The place is well heated. Mobility is all I lack, so I do exercises and pace up and down my cell with the window open. ...

We've now been waiting for each other for almost two years, dearest Maria. Don't lose heart! I'm glad you're with my parents. Give my fondest love to your mother and the whole family. Here are another few verses that have occurred to me in recent nights. They're my Christmas greeting to you, my parents, and my brothers and sisters.

By kindly, faithful, tranquil powers surrounded
that wonderfully shield me and console,
thus will I share these days with you in spirit
and enter on a new year with you all.

Although the old year still our hearts oppresses,
and still of evil times we bear the weight,
O Lord, bestow upon us that salvation
for which our troubled souls thou didst create.

If thou should offer us the cup of sorrow,
the bitter, brimming chalice we'll withstand
and thankfully accept it, never flinching,
from out thy righteous and beloved hand.

But if it be thy will once more to let us
delight in this world and its bright sunshine,
then shall we all these bygone days remember,
then shall our lives be absolutely thine.

The candles brought by thee into our darkness,
let them today burn clear and warm and bright,
and bring us, if thou wilt, once more together!
Thy light, we know it well, shines in the night.

Now, when in deepest silence we're enfolded,
permit us, Lord, to hear thy children raise,
from that world which, unseen, lies round about us,
their lofty and exalted hymn of praise.

By kindly powers so wondrously protected
we wait with confidence, befall what may.
We are with God at night and in the morning,
and, just as certainly, on each new day.

In great love and gratitude to you, my parents, and my
brothers and sisters.
I embrace you.

Yours, Dietrich

As the Red Army launched its offensive in the east, Maria left Berlin to help her mother prepare to leave Pätzig. On February 3, Berlin sustained its heaviest air raid of the war. The Central State Security Bureau was damaged; on February 7, Bonhoeffer and other security prisoners were transferred to the Buchenwald Concentration Camp. On April 3, the prisoners were moved further south to Schönberg in the Bavarian Forest, and by April 7 Bonhoeffer was transported to Flossenbürg, where he and five others were hanged the next morning. Survivors testify that Bonhoeffer spent his last months in prayer and encouragement of his fellow-prisoners. His message sent to the Anglican Bishop of Chichester was 'This is the end - for me, the beginning of life.'[10] Within a month of Bonhoeffer's execution, the German forces had surrendered to the Allies.

Maria had unsuccessfully tried to find Bonhoeffer at Flossenbürg. She did not learn of his death until June, after the war was over. After the war, Maria maintained her contact with the Bonhoeffers and treasured her correspondence with Dietrich. A friend of Dietrich's in America helped her come to the United States on a scholarship to Bryn Mawr. She remained in America and became an accomplished corporate mathematician as well as a devoted mother of two sons, though her two marriages ended in divorce.

During her life, Maria was always reluctant to publish Bonhoeffer's letters to her. A few years before her death, she wrote her sister Ruth-Alice, 'You're right in saying that one must wait for things and give them time to mature. It always surprises me how incredibly sensitive I am in regard to Dietrich and my relationship with him.'[11] In 1976, Maria attended an international conference in Geneva to mark the anniversary of Dietrich Bonhoeffer's seventieth birthday. Here she met theologians from around the world who had been influenced by Bonhoeffer, as well as

---

10   Geffrey B. Kelly, 'The Life and Death of a Modern Martyr,' *Christian History*, Issue 52 (Vol. X, No. 4,) 17.

11   *Love Letters from Cell 92*, 304

Bonhoeffer's old friends from the Finkenwalde Seminary. Maria's dignified, confident manner impressed many at the conference, and Maria herself was deeply moved, as she wrote her sister: 'The whole Geneva experience affected me far more than I would ever have thought possible. ... It was a very cheerful gathering and, for that reason, absolutely appropriate to Dietrich.'[12] Always vivacious and caring of others, Maria died of cancer in 1977.

12 *Love Letters from Cell 92* ,306.

CHRISTOPHER

AND

MARY LOVE

(1618-1651)

'God hath put heaven in thee before He hath taken thee to heaven.'
Mary Love

Christopher Love was a pastor in London during the English Civil War. He was a prolific writer who published numerous works, all written to help Christians grow in grace and learn the usefulness of biblical theology. He had opposed the execution of King Charles I and the establishment of Oliver Cromwell as Lord Protector. In 1651, Love and six other prominent ministers were accused of high treason, charged with plotting the overthrow of Cromwell and the reinstatement of the monarchy under Charles II. Though the other ministers were released after a brief imprisonment, Love remained in the Tower of London and was sentenced to be executed. Mary Love, Christopher's wife of sixteen years, worked tirelessly to have her husband released. The letters between Christopher and Mary Love reveal a passionate love and Christian bond with roots in, and eyes on, eternity.

July 14, 1651

Before I write a word further, I beseech thee think not that it is thy wife but a friend now that writes to thee. I hope thou hast freely given up thy wife and children to God, who hath said in Jeremiah 49:11, 'Leave thy fatherless children, I will preserve them alive, and let thy widow trust in me.' Thy Maker will be my husband, and a Father to thy children. O that the Lord would keep thee from having one troubled thought for thy relations. I desire freely to give thee up into thy Father's hands, and not only look upon it as a crown of glory for thee to die for Christ, but as an honor to me that I should have a husband to leave for Christ.

I dare not speak to thee, nor have a thought within my own heart of my unspeakable loss, but wholly keep my eye fixed upon thy inexpressible and inconceivable gain. Thou leavest but a sinful, mortal wife to be everlastingly married to the Lord of glory. Thou leavest but children, brothers, and sisters to go to the Lord Jesus, thy eldest Brother. Thou leavest friends on earth to go to the enjoyment of saints and angels, and the spirits of just men made perfect in glory. Thou dost but leave earth for heaven and changest a prison for a palace. And if natural affections should begin to arise, I hope that spirit of grace that is within thee will quell them, knowing that all things here below are but dung and dross in comparison of those things that are above. I know thou keepest thine eye fixed on the hope of glory, which makes thy feet trample on the loss of earth.

My dear, I know God hath not only prepared glory for thee, and thee for it, but I am persuaded that He will sweeten the way for thee to come to the enjoyment of it. When thou art putting on thy clothes that morning, O think, 'I am now putting on my wedding garments to go to be everlastingly married to my Redeemer.'

When the messenger of death comes to thee, let him not seem dreadful to thee, but look on him as a messenger that brings thee tidings of eternal life. When thou goest up the scaffold, think (as thou saidst to me) that it is but thy fiery chariot to carry thee up to thy Father's house.

And when thou layest down thy precious head to receive thy Father's stroke, remember what thou saidst to me: Though thy head was severed from thy body, yet in a moment thy soul should be united to thy Head, the Lord Jesus, in heaven. And though it may seem something bitter, that by the hands of men we are parted a little sooner than otherwise we might have been, yet let us consider that it is the decree and will of our Father, and it will not be long ere we shall enjoy one another in heaven again.

Let us comfort one another with these sayings. Be comforted, my dear heart. It is but a little stroke and thou shalt be there where the weary shall be at rest and where the wicked shall cease from troubling. Remember that thou mayest eat thy dinner with bitter herbs, yet thou shalt have a sweet supper with Christ that night. My dear, by what I write unto thee, I do not hereby undertake to teach thee; for these comforts I have received from the Lord by thee. I shall write no more, nor trouble thee any further, but commit thee into the arms of God with whom ere long thee and I shall be.

Farewell, my dear. I shall never see thy face more till we both behold the face of the Lord Jesus at that great day.

Mary Love[1]

From the Tower of London on the Lord's Day
More Dear to me than Ever,

It adds to my rejoicing that I have so good and gracious wife to part with for the Lord Jesus. In thy grief, I have been grieved; but in thy joy I have been comforted. Surely, nature could never help thee to bear so heavy a stroke with so much

---

1   Don Kistler, *A Spectacle unto God: The Life and Death of Christopher Love (1618-1651)*. Soli Deo Gloria Publications, 1998, 1-3.

silence and submission to the hand of God! Oh, dearest, every line which thou writest gladdeneth my heart. I dare not think that there is such a creature has More Love in the world. For Kit and Mall [the two living children], I can think of them without trouble, leaving them to so good a God and so good a mother.

Be comforted concerning thy husband, who may more honor God in his death than in his life. The will of the Lord be done; he is fully satisfied with the hand of God. Though there is but little between him and death, he knows there is but little between him and heaven, and that ravisheth his heart.

The Lord bless and requite thee for thy wise and good counsel. Thou hast prevented me; the very things I thought to have written to thee, thou hast written to me. I have had more comfort from thy gracious letters than from all the counsel I have had from any else in the world. Well, be assured, we shall meet in heaven. I rest till I rest in heaven, thy dying but comforted friend,

Christopher Love[2]

August 21, 1651 [the day before Christopher's execution]
My Heavenly Dear,

I call thee so because God hath put heaven into thee before He hath taken thee to heaven. Thou now beholdest God, Christ and glory as in a glass; but tomorrow, heaven's gates will be opened and thou shalt be in the full enjoyment of all those glories which eye hath not seen, nor ear heard, neither can the heart of man understand. God hath now swallowed up thy heart in the thoughts of heaven, but ere long thou shalt be swallowed up in the enjoyment of heaven. And no marvel there should be such quietness and calmness in thy spirit while thou art sailing in this tempestuous sea, because

2   *Spectacle unto God*, 99.

thou perceivest by the eye of faith a haven of rest where thou shalt be richly laden with all the glories of heaven. O lift up thy heart with joy when thou layest thy dear head on the block in the thought of this: that thou are laying thy head to rest in thy Father's bosom which, when thou dost awake, shall be crowned not with an earthly fading crown but with a heavenly eternal crown of glory.

And be not discouraged when thou shalt see a guard of soldiers triumphing with their trumpets about thee, but lift up thy head and thou shalt behold God with a guard of His holy angels, triumphing to receive thee to glory. Be not dismayed at the scoffs and reproaches that thou mayest meet with in thy short way to heaven, for be assured that God will not only glorify thy body and soul in heaven but He will also make the memory of thee to be glorious on earth!

O let not one troubled thought for thy wife and babes arise within thee. Thy God will be our God and our portion. He will be a husband to thy widow and a father to thy children; the grace of thy God will be sufficient for us.

Now my dear, I desire willingly and cheerfully to resign my right in thee to thy Father and my father, who hath the greatest interest in thee. And confident I am, though men have separated us for a time yet our God will ere long bring us together again where we shall eternally enjoy one another, never to part more. O let me hear how God bears up thy heart, and let me taste of those comforts that support thee, that they may be as pillars of marble to bear up my sinking spirit. I can write no more. Farewell, farewell, my dear, till we meet there where we shall never bid farewell more; till which time I leave thee in the bosom of a loving, tender-hearted Father. And so I rest till I shall forever rest in heaven,

Mary Love[3]

---

3   *Spectacle unto God*, 84-85.

JOHN NEWTON
AND
MARY NEWTON

John Newton

(1725-1807)

Mary Newton

(1729-1790)

'Long experience and much observation have convinced me, that the marriage state, when properly formed and prudently conducted, affords the nearest approach to happiness (of a merely temporal kind) that can be attained in this uncertain world. ...'

John Newton

Today John Newton is best known for his inspiring hymn 'Amazing Grace'; in his own day he was one of England's most prominent preachers. Before his conversion, Newton's life had become so debauched, irreverent, and immoral that even his fellow-sailors were shocked by his conduct and coarse speech. Yet, God in His grace reached down and redeemed John Newton, transformed his life, and made him a preacher of the Gospel. Newton never ceased to be amazed at God's work in his life. He frequently admitted that God had used his passionate love for his wife Mary as a motive and means for his spiritual betterment.

John Newton's and Mary Catlett's mothers had been the best of friends and, when the two children were infants, had talked about them marrying each other. But Newton's mother died when John was seven, and when his father remarried, the Catletts and Newtons drifted apart. John's father was a sea captain, and when John was eleven, his father was already taking him to sea with him. When John was seventeen, his father made arrangements for him to go to Jamaica and help manage a slave plantation there. Before he left, however, the Catletts had invited John for a visit. He had not seen the family since his mother's death and decided to visit them. When seventeen-year-old John laid eyes on Mary, the oldest of the Catlett children, he lost his heart. Over twenty years later he wrote

> Almost at the first sight of the girl (for she was then under fourteen) I felt an affection for her, which never abated or lost its influence a single moment in my heart. In degree, it equaled all that the writers of romance have imagined; in duration it was unalterable.
>
> I soon lost all sense of religion, and became deaf to the remonstrances of conscience. But none of the misery I experienced ever banished her a single hour from my waking thoughts for seven years following. ...
>
> When I later made shipwreck of faith, hope, and conscience, my love to this person was the only remaining principle which in any degree took their place. The bare possibility of seeing her again was the only means of restraining me from the most horrid designs against myself and others.[1]

Later in life, John was amazed that he was so strongly attached to Mary as a young person. His life at that time was a rebellious one, and his passion for Mary was the only element of purity in his life. After their marriage, John wrote Mary while at sea:

> How wonderful, that when we were both so young, an impression should be made upon my mind, almost at first sight, which neither distance, nor absence, nor all my sufferings, nor even all the licentiousness and folly I afterward ran into, could obliterate!

1   John Newton, *Out of the Depths*. Grand Rapids, Michigan: Kregel Publications, 1990. (Newton's autobiography was first published in 1764.)

I know not at first which ailed me. I was uneasy when you were absent, yet when you were present I scarcely durst look at you. If I attempted to speak, I trembled and was confused. My love made me stupid at first. I could not bear to leave you; but once and again broke my engagements, and disappointed my father's aim to settle me in life, rather than be banished far from you.[2]

John's first meeting with Mary was the first of several times he deserted his work to be with her. His visit with the Catletts stretched from three days to three weeks, and the ship for Jamaica left without him. John couldn't bear the thought of going to Jamaica and not seeing Mary for five years! His father was able to find him a position on a merchant ship, but John's rebelliousness, insolence, and disobedience soon caused him to be demoted to a common sailor. His lowered position did not raise him in the eyes of Mary's family, yet John's love remained unchanged. Again overstaying his leave from his ship to be with Mary, in 1744 John was impressed[3] into service on the *Harwich*, a man-of-war engaged in the war with France. By the next year, he transferred to a merchant ship bound for Africa in the slave trade. John's life seemed to be drifting farther and farther from Mary, and he despaired of ever seeing her again. He became a free-thinker, rejecting the Scriptures and the Christian truths once learned from his mother.

For a time he lived on the African coast - sick with fever, hungry, ill-clothed, and often despairing of life itself. Finally the ship *Greyhound*, captained by Joseph Manesty, a friend of John's father, found out about John's whereabouts and picked him up to take him back to England. When John thought of England, he thought of Mary, and his hopes began to rise, though in his unprincipled life he was totally unworthy of her. During a storm

---

2   John Newton to Mary. August 28, 1750 in *Letters to a Wife*. Philadelphia: William Young, 1797. All quotes from Newton's letters are from this work.

3   The word 'pressed' is probably the better term to use today. At the time, sailors forced into service on ship were 'impressed'.

at sea, however, when John and all aboard despaired of life, the Scriptures John had once learned at his mother's knee returned to his mind, and he began to have hope that Jesus could deliver him, dreadful sinner that he was. For the first time in years, John sought the Lord in prayer, and on March 21, 1748, a date Newton remembered yearly for the rest of his life, as Newton wrote, 'the Lord sent from on high and delivered me out of deep waters.'

When John returned to England that May, he saw Mary only briefly in London, and he was too tongue-tied to speak to her of matters so near his heart. He wrote her a letter proposing marriage. Though her reply was cautious, it was not a refusal, and John's spirit soared: 'Then, my dearest M[ary], on that very day, I began to live indeed, and to act, in all my concerns, with a spirit and firmness to which I before was a stranger. My next voyage, though troublesome enough, yet, enlivened by the hopes you had given me, was to be light and easy.'[4]

On the next voyage John began to grow as a young Christian, seeking the Lord in prayer and reading and meditating on the Scriptures. When he returned to England, John and Mary were married on February 1, 1750. Their life together for the next forty years was filled with a boundless love; John always recognized this special love was among the greatest of the gifts of Providence.

In 1793, three years after Mary's death, John published a two-volume collection of letters he had sent to Mary over the years. In the preface, he gave four reasons for publishing the letters: first, to give public testimony of thanks to God for such a treasure as his wife, 'for uniting our hearts by such tender ties, and for continuing her to me for so long'; second, as a monument of respect and gratitude to her memory since, 'She was my pleasing companion, my most affectionate friend, my judicious counselor'; third, to show by example 'that marriage, when the parties are united by affection, and the general conduct is governed by religion and prudence, is not only an honorable but a comfortable state'; and

---

4   *Letters to a Wife.* September 2, 1750.

finally, to be an example and warning to others who set out to satisfy their creature comforts.

After his marriage, John was captain of his own ship and would have to be separated from Mary for long months at a time. While John was in Liverpool preparing for the voyage, the two corresponded constantly. At sea John wrote two or three times a week, even though there might not be a way of sending the letters home for six or eight months.

Though captain of a slave ship involved in the triangular slave trade between Africa, England, and the Americas, Newton at this time was not particularly bothered by its evils, though later in life he would encourage the abolition of slavery and enlist William Wilberforce in the antislavery fight. His letters overflow with love for his new bride and a desire to be all that his God wants him to be.

The printed letters do not contain the salutation or ending of the letters, but John's usual address was 'My dearest charming Polly' (as Mary was often called), 'My dearest, charming, obliging Polly,' or 'My dearest charmer'. His letters usually ended with 'your most affectionate and obliged husband and admirer, J. Newton.'

> July 31 [1750] from Liverpool
> If my dearest M[ary] will permit me to offer my best advice, and which I propose as a rule to myself - it is this - To endeavor to cast all our care upon Him, who has promised to care for us, if we will but put our trust in him.[5] I long attempted to apply the specious maxims of philosophy, to soften the cares and trials of life, but I find them ineffectual and false. ... Yet I am very sure, that under this aggravated circumstance of separation from you, I shall be miserable and without support, if religion did not assist me with noble and more powerful motives of consolation. I go from you with the less regret, because I leave you in the hands of Him who is able, and I trust willing to preserve you from all evil, and to make everything easy to you. And I look forward to

---

5   I Peter 5:7.

the various scenes of my intended voyage with cheerfulness, because I am sensible that in the most remote inhospitable climes, a protecting Providence will surround me. ...

After being delayed by a fierce storm at sea, Newton wrote to Mary of the trouble as an example of the preservation by Providence.

Ramsay, Isle of Man,[6] 24 August [1750]
I readily inform you of the danger we have been in, now it is happily over, and hope you will not be alarmed because I am still liable to the like, but rather be comforted with the thought that in the greatest difficulties the same Great Deliverer is always present. The winds and the seas obey him. I endeavor, in every scene of distress, to recollect the seasons in my past life, in which, when I have given myself up for lost, I have been unexpectedly relieved. Instances of this kind have been frequent with me, some of them as remarkable as any that have been recorded. Particularly my preservation in the *Greyhound* in the year 48, which can only be accounted for by an immediate and almost miraculous interposition of Divine Providence.[7]

Rio Junque, January [1751]
When I meet with anything cross, or contrary to my wish, I dare not now complain; because in gaining you I secured the principal aim of my life; a real good, which if set in opposition to the little disappointments I meet with from without, outweighs them all. Nor need I envy others their wealth or prosperity, when it is a thousand to one if any of them have such a dear M[ary] as I can call my own. I should therefore be sorry to change with the very best of them, in all points, or to part with a small portion of your regard for any worldly consideration. ...

---

6   The Isle of Man is an island, a sovereign country located in the Irish Sea. On a clear day Scotland, Ireland, England and Wales can all be seen from its shores.

7   This was the time when it seemed all on board would be lost. It was during this storm that Newton began to recall the Scriptures learned as a youth and was brought to Christ.

I shall never forget, and you doubtless will remember, the evening when you first gave me your hand, as an earnest of what has since followed. How I sat stupid and speechless for some minutes, and I believe a little embarrassed you by my awkwardness. My heart was so full, it beat and trembled to that degree, that I knew not how to get a word out. I hope I shall never entertain a fainter sense of the invaluable present you then made me; though a greater intimacy has since restored to me the use of my tongue.

Shebar, 20 February [1751]

Last night (which made it a remarkable night) I dreamed of you. Methought we were walking together and mutually hearing and relating many things which had occurred since our parting. It was a pleasing illusion; but at day-light the noise of the people over my head broke the charm, and reminded me that for a time I must submit to a different scene. But I seemed more refreshed by my dream than I should have been by a long sleep.

I sometimes wonder that my sleeping fancy does not oftener transport me to you. Were it true, as some suppose, that our dreams are usually influenced by our employment when awake, I should surely dream of you always. For my attention is so seldom engaged by the most pressing business, as to exclude the thoughts of you five minutes at a time. Perhaps my mind, being so taken up with you when I am awake, is glad to take the opportunity of sleeping when my body does. Yet I well remember that when I first loved you I dreamed of you, night after night, for near three months successively; though I certainly could not have half the regard for you then that I have now.

Shebar, March 22 [1751]

A desire of rendering myself agreeable to you has long been a motive of my conduct. This I may well [call] my <u>ruling</u>

<u>passion</u>. I was changeable as the weather, till my regard for you fixed me, and collected all my aims to the single point of gaining you. Then my faculties, which before were remiss, were roused, and indolence gave way to application. It has been observed, that those who have wearied themselves in vainly searching for the Philosopher's stone,[8] have often found out useful things which they had no thought of seeking. So I, in the pursuit of the methods by which I hoped to influence you, obtained unawares advantages of another kind. The desire of pleasing you insensibly made me more acceptable to others.

Newton responds to Mary's warning to be careful for his life for her sake.

Antigua,[9] July 5 [1751]
God only knows which of us must depart first, but it is probable one must survive the knowledge of the other's death. If it should be my lot, I cannot tell how I should be able to bear it; but I would wish our love to be so regulated, that neither of us should be rendered miserable by a separation; but rather be supported by a well grounded hope, that a few more rolling years would reunite us never more to part. In a world liable to such unexpected and unavoidable changes, there is no probability of being happy, even in the enjoyment of our own wishes, unless we hold them in subordination to the will and wisdom of God, who is the author and giver of every blessing.

Antigua, August 4 [1751]
... A love like mine, is calculated for all seasons and changes; equally suited to enlarge the advantages of prosperity beyond

---

8   Alchemists were always looking for the Philosopher's stone, a substance supposed to change other metals into gold or silver.

9   An island of the Lesser Antilles in the Caribbean Sea.

the comprehension of a stranger, and to gild the uneasy hours of pain and trouble. I may lose money, health, liberty, or limbs, but while it pleases God to preserve my memory, nothing can rob me of the consciousness that you are mine, and that I am favored with the dearest place in your heart. ... Adieu, my dearest, Believe me to be almost continually praying for you and studying how to improve myself, ...

At Sea, August 14 [1751]

... I suppose most people when entering the marriage state promise themselves much satisfaction; and I am afraid very many are greatly disappointed. Why has it been otherwise with me? How was it, that at a time when I was mistaken and wrong in every other part of my conduct, I should direct my address to perhaps the only one in the sphere of my acquaintance who could make me happy? Undoubtedly the hand of God was in it. ... Besides my other obligations, I must always consider you as the principal instrument employed by Providence to wean me from those errors and evils, which otherwise must have soon issued in my destruction. ... I shall have reason, with my dying breath, to bless God for the influence you have had over me.

Looking on his past, Newton could not help but rest easy in all circumstances, regardless of how difficult. After all, hadn't God blessed his life with preservation when he was in wickedness and rebellion? If God brought such blessing then, how much more now that he was seeking to follow him!

September 5th [1751]

I entered upon this voyage with little anxiety, though I well knew it would expose me to many dangers, because I had been protected before, and brought through the like unhurt. I parted from you with grief, it is true, and yet with a degree of cheerfulness, because I trusted that he who brought us together so much beyond my expectations and deserts would restore us to each other again at a proper time and for the same reason, my heart now exults in the hope that the time is nearly approaching. ...

At Sea, October 3 [1751]

What a tasteless unpleasant voyage would this have been if you had not secured my happiness before I came out, and given me something to remember, and something to hope for, that has supported me at all times: and yet you denied me at first, with so grave a face, and had such absolute command over me, that I had almost taken you at your word. ...

I then began to press my point more closely, till you actually yielded, and gave me your hand in consent; which though I had been so long entreating for, I could not receive without trembling and surprise. I could hardly think myself awake. I never till then was sensible of the force of my love; and I slept that night with a content and sweetness which I had not known before. I often recollect these circumstances, and the much ado I made about you before marriage, to make me careful that my behavior now may be suitable to my former professions. But, I thank God, it does not require much care or pains, for to do all in my power to please and oblige you, seems as natural to me as to breathe.

Newton's ship arrived at Liverpool October 8, but he was unable to reach Mary until November 2. By April he had to return to Liverpool and prepare to launch a new ship on his second voyage. The *African* set out for Africa on June 30. This was to prove the most dangerous of Newton's voyages. Sickness, mutiny among his men, slave rebellion, and false accusations made against him all plagued the journey. Though Newton's journal clearly reveals his trials, these difficulties are not mentioned in his letters to Mary.

On this voyage John held to a strict discipline of prayer, reading, and study, in addition to his duties as ship captain. His

letters show an increasing concern for his and Mary's spiritual
growth and development.

June 30 [1752]

The first thing I shall say is I am really easy. Though I have no
relish for mirth, my mind is at peace. The knowledge of your
love, the recollection of the happy time I have passed with
you, and the powerful considerations of a more serious kind,
which I have often repeated to you, have all the effect upon
me that you could wish. And I assure you the resolution you
have shown has no small influence, both as an example, and
in giving me hope that you will strive to be composed, and
to depend, with me, upon the good Providence which has
already done so much for us. ... May the good and gracious
God bless and preserve you. Remember my last advice. Be
patient and thankful, and expect me, at the best time, to
return and be happy with you again.

At Sea, 11 July [1752]

I have almost dismissed my fear upon your account, for
I have so often recommended and resigned you to the
protection of God, that I seldom doubt of his special care
over you. But I have bound myself in a strict promise, ... that
when He shall be pleased to bring us together again in peace,
we will both endeavour to shew gratitude by our conduct,
as well as to express it in words. In the mean while, it is one
of my daily and nightly petitions, that he may teach us to
extract a real good out of these our painful separations, by
improving the occasion to the increasing and fixing our best
affections on himself. From his favour and goodness our
blessings, and even our mutual love, proceeds.

At Sea, 24 July [1752]

I know you have thought of me to-day, because it is my
birth-day. I have likewise observed it. I would willingly grow
wiser and better, as I grow older, every year. I have now

lived twenty-seven years, but how few things have I done really worthy of life, unless I am allowed to consider the instances in which I have endeavoured to shew my affection and gratitude to you ... and my prayer and wish for you is, that we may be both of one mind, and prove helps to each other. ... I continue to conceive most of my prayers in the plural number, as when we were together; for every desirable good that I can ask for myself, I am equally solicitous that you should be a sharer in.

At Sea, 7 August [1752]

... when I indulge myself with a particular thought of you, it usually carries me on farther, and brings me upon my knees to bless the Lord, for giving me such a treasure, and to pray for your peace and welfare. ... When thus engaged, my fears subside, my impatience of your absence changes into a resignation full of hope, and every anxious uneasy thought is lulled to rest. ...

At Sea, 11 August [1752]

... when I take up my pen, and begin to consider what I shall say, I am led to think of the goodness of God, who has made you mine, and given me a heart to value you. Thus my love to you, and my gratitude to him, cannot be separated. ... All other love, that is not connected with a dependence on God, must be precarious. To this want, I attribute many unhappy marriages. ...

Newton's letter continued to note that the world is subjected to vanity so that we can see that the great aim of this life is to prepare for another. Those who learn to submit to the trials of life can avoid bitterness, delighting in the Lord's wisdom and guidance. But, those who so depend on each other that they neglect the common preserver bring judgment upon themselves (sickness, suffering, and death).

In a Sabbath set aside for the Lord, Newton spent the morning in reviewing the various mercies he had received. The afternoon was spent in prayer with his God.

> Mana, 1 December [1752]
>
> [In my prayers] Oh! how I remember you! My first acknowledgments are for your love, and that you are mine ... My prayers for you are, for your health, peace, and satisfaction ... but above all for your progress in religion, and that you may have a prospect of happiness, independent of all earthly comforts, and superior to them. So disinterested is my love, that ... I tremble at the thought of being over-regarded, or that you should wholly rest your peace upon such a wretched feeble prop as I am. A love with all our heart, and mind, and soul, and strength (such, I fear, ours has too much been to each other) can be only due to our maker and great benefactor.

On August 29, 1753, the *African* arrived in Liverpool, ending Newton's second voyage as captain. The ship had brought 207 slaves to the southern colonies in America and returned to England with a cargo of cotton, sugar, and rum. By the end of October, John again was aboard the *African* headed for West Africa. Newton's letters to Mary continued to reflect his concern for their mutual spiritual growth.

> At Sea, 23 November [1753]
>
> You will not be displeased with me for saying, that though you are dearer to me than the aggregate of all earthly comforts, I wish to limit my passion within those bounds which God has appointed. Our love to each other ought to lead us to love him supremely, who is the author and source of all the good we possess or hope for. It is to him we owe that happiness in a marriage state which so many seek in vain, some of whom set out with such hopes and prospects,

that their disappointments can be deduced for no other cause, than having placed that high regard on a creature which is only due to the Creator. He therefore withholds his blessing (without which no union can subsist) and their expectations, of course, end in ... an indifference. ...

Rio Junk[10] 17 January [1754]

In the midst of a thousand hurries, and avocations, I must steal a few minutes, to converse with you. I have been almost wearied today with noise, heat, smoke, and business; but when I think of you, the inconvenience is gone. Which of your learned philosophers can define this wonderful, transforming thing, called Love, that so infuses a degree of pleasure into trouble and disquiet?

The ship that is to take my packet, is upon the point of sailing. I must wind up all, with fervent prayers, that it may please the Lord, the giver of all good, to preserve us in peace and dependence, during the appointed term of our separation; and in the good hour, to give us a happy meeting; and that we may learn to wait for that time with patience, with more than patience, with thankfulness that our prospects are only delayed ... and not wholly cut off. ... Above all, I pray, that in every season of life, we may prepare for what we know must, sooner or later, take place. That we may believe, and act, on the principles of the gospel, to the glory of our Maker and Redeemer here, and then we shall be happy for ever hereafter, beyond the reach of sorrow or pain, and never more know, what it is to part.

Rio Sestors, 25 January [1754]

I expected, before I left England, that the present voyage would not prove successful, in point of profit. I was not mistaken. I shall hardly reach the half of my last year's purchase. I hope the vessel I have bought, to trade after I am

---

10   Newton is not always consistent in his spelling of places on the African coast; previously he had spelled this Rio Junque.

gone, may secure the owners [sic] interest; but my own part of the affair, will probably be moderate enough.

If a sigh should escape you on this account, I beg you to recollect yourself, and not indulge a second. Remember, that this failure in dirty money matters, is the only abatement we have hitherto met with; and that in other respects, we have as much the advantage, of those who are [in] the world, as we fall short of them in riches. We have blessings, which riches cannot purchase, nor compensate for the want of. And I see much cause for thankfulness, that things are no worse. We want for nothing at present, and for the future, we may safely rely on the good Providence, that has done so much for us already. ...

In an earlier part of the following letter, John congratulates Mary on her birthday and recalls that as children their mothers had been friends and talked about them growing up to become man and wife. Although the relationship between the families was broken off for years, when he saw her again, he was drawn to her, yet he knew not how or why he loved her. His friends and hers advised against the match!

2 February [1754]

I have abundant reason to praise the Lord that before I had been four years in the world, he should provide for me, in you, the greatest blessing of my life with which he purposed to enhance and crown all his many mercies to me; and that you might be in time as a guardian angel, to preserve me from ruin. I desire to praise him for all the goodness which has followed you from the hour I am commemorating to this day; for the great protection which preserved you for me, through your early years; for your health and satisfaction since you have been mine; and for enabling me, thus far, to answer the trust you have reposed in me. And I humbly pray, that the affections and engagements may be preserved inviolate between ourselves, and in a proper subordination to what we owe to him, the great Lord of all.

Settra Crue, 6 February [1754]

... I consider our union as a peculiar effect and gift of an indulgent Providence, and therefore as a talent to be improved to higher ends,[11] to the promoting his will and service upon earth, and to the assisting each other to prepare for an eternal state, to which a few years at the farthest will introduce us. Were these points wholly neglected, however great our satisfaction might be for the present, it would be better never to have seen each other; since the time must come when, of all the endearments of our connection, nothing will remain, but the consciousness how greatly we were favored, and how we improved the favours we possessed. ...

At Sea, 13 July [1754]

Of all the authors I have read, who have occasionally treated of a married life, and of the inadvertencies on both sides, by which it is too often rendered unhappy; I do not remember one, who has touched upon the great evil of all; I mean our wretched propensity, to lay the foundation of our proposed happiness, independent of God. If we are happy in a mutual affection when we set out, we are too apt to think, that nothing more is wanting; and to suppose our own prudence and good judgment, sufficient to carry us on the end. But that is not so, in fact, we have daily proof from the example of numbers, who notwithstanding a sincere regard to each at first, and the advantages of good sense, and good temper, in general, yet by some hidden causes, gradually become cool, and indifferent; and at length, burdensome, perhaps hateful to each other. This event is often noticed, and excites surprise, because few can properly account for it. ...

It is an undoubted truth, that the Most High God, who is ever present with, and over his creatures, is the author,

---

11 Newton alludes here to the parable of the talents in Matthew 25:14-30. Like the talents in the parable, Newton believed God gave him and Mary a love and union which should be invested for the Lord's glory.

and giver of all that is agreeable, or comfortable to us, in the world. We cannot be easy in ourselves, or acceptable to others, but by his favour; and therefore, when we presume to use his creative comforts, without consulting and acknowledging him in them, his honour is concerned to disappoint us. Dreaming of sure satisfaction, in the prosecution, or enjoyment of our own desires, we do but imitate the builders of Babel, who said, Go to, let us build a tower, to get ourselves a name. So we too often when circumstances smile upon us, vainly think of securing happiness upon earth; a sensual happiness, and on all earth that stands accursed, and subject to vanity, for our sins. In every state and scene of life, there are instances of this folly; but perhaps it is in no one, more insinuating and plausible, than in the commencement of marriage between those whose hearts are united. But alas! God looks down upon such short-sighted projections, as he did upon those of old. He pours contempt on their design; he divides their language; he permits separate views and interests to rise in their minds; their fair scheme of happiness degenerates into confusion, and they are left under the reproach, of having begun to build, what they will never be able to finish ... neglecting to own and to seek God in their concerns, he has refused them that blessing, without which no union can subsist. ...

Oh may we adore him, who provided us for each other; who brought us together, and has spared us so long! May we love each other till death, yea, I hope in a future state beyond death! And in order to this, may we, in the first place, love him with all our heart, and soul, and strength, who first loved us, to renew our forfeited title, to the good things of both worlds, and to wash us from our sins in his blood. This was love indeed! Where were the sensibility and ingenuousness of spirit which we sometimes think we possess, that this unspeakable lover of souls has been no more noticed, no more admired and beloved by us hitherto.

Lord! make us partakers of thy divine nature: for thou art Love!

In August the *African* returned to Liverpool, and John was again able to enjoy a few months with Mary. By November, however, the *Bee* was ready to sail for Africa with Newton in charge of his fourth voyage. A few days before the *Bee* was to sail, John and Mary were enjoying tea together in the Liverpool home of Captain and Mrs Manesty, when John slumped to the floor. For an hour he showed no signs of life except breathing, and Mary herself fainted from the shock. John was carried to his bed with dizziness and headaches but did recover. The doctors diagnosed an apoplectic fit and advised against his returning to sea. By this way John left the sailing life; he resigned two days before the *Bee* sailed. Mary had been dealt a severe blow when John lay as dead, and she grew weaker and weaker. Hoping that familiar surroundings would improve her, John took Mary to her home in Chatham. There during the next eleven months she slowly recovered. For the remainder of her life Mary would periodically suffer illness for five to six months at a time; the rest of the time she was in perfect health.

Chatham was near London, and John would frequently go to London to be under the ministry of George Whitefield and other evangelical preachers. This was the time when the evangelical revival was sweeping the country.

In August, Captain Manesty obtained John the appointment of Tide Surveyor for Liverpool. Smuggling was rampant, and John's duty was to check the incoming vessels. Mary was not yet well enough to make the journey to Liverpool, so John and Mary were again separated; the letter writing resumed.

Liverpool, 26 August [1755][12]

... I have hardly known you allow, till now, that you were enabled to pray. We may praise God, in that pain or sickness,

---

12   It was during her severe illness that Mary seemed to learn genuinely to pray.

however severe, which teaches us, in good earnest, to call upon Him. You have been in trouble, you called upon him, and he has delivered you, according to his word. What shall we render to Him for all His mercies! Alas, we are poor, and we can render nothing of our own. But he will not despise the efforts of a thankful heart. ...

Liverpool, 9 September [1755]

... When it shall please God to bring us together again, I hope we shall strengthen each other's hands. Let us pray for this while we are separated, that we may not be left anymore to live to ourselves, but to him; and may look upwards and forwards, to be prepared for the next trial; for sooner or later more will come. ...

... I want nothing that this world can afford to amend my situation, but to have my dearest M[ary] with me, and for this, the Lord's time will be the best.

Liverpool, 12 September [1755]

... Most of my leisure this week will be taken up with Mr. Wh[itefiel]d,[13] which, as it is an occasional interruption, and from which I hope both for comfort and benefit, I think you will excuse. He came to town on Wednesday, preached on that evening twice yesterday and so will continue preaching twice a day while he stays. We shall try to keep him till Monday, though he says he never was in a place where he had so little encouragement to stay as here. I made myself known to him the first night, went to see him, and conversed with him the next morning, when he invited me to supper. I went home with him from the preaching, and staid [sic] till ten o'clock. ... May the Lord yet give him to see that his labour of love amongst us, is not in vain. But surely this is the most

---

13   George Whitefield was the great evangelist of the eighteenth-century revival in England and America. Often co-operating with the Wesleys in reaching the unchurched masses, Whitefield was noted for the spiritual power of his oratory to move the hearts of his hearers.

unconcerned town for its [spirituality in] the kingdom. I hope he is sent to awaken some of the people out of their false peace. However he is, as was formerly, very helpful to me.[14] He warms my heart, makes me more indifferent to cares and crosses, and strengthens my faith. I find you are making acquaintance with Mr. M.[15] Well, go on, I hope you will leave London soon, or you will be thought as singular as your husband. To speak seriously, it makes my heart glad to see in you one mark of a real believer, in that you love the ministers and people of the Lord, and are not offended with the gospel, which is a stumbling-block and rock of offense to many. May he carry on his work, and hold you up in knowledge, faith, and much assurance. Amen. Think of me, as always thinking of you and praying for you.

Liverpool, 16 September [1755]
Mr. W[hitefield] left us yesterday morning, I accompanied him on foot a little way out of town, till the chaise overtook us. I have had more of his company than [I] would have [been able to share] at London, in a twelve-month. I heard him preach nine times, supped with him three times, and dined with him once at Mr. F-'s and on Sunday he dined with me. I cannot say how much I esteem him, and hope to my dying day I shall have reason to bless God on his behalf. Having never been here before but one night, he was not known or regarded by the fashionable folks, though several of them went to hear him. But many of the poorer sort are inquiring after him with tears.

I commenced acquaintance yesterday with a good man, who lately lost his wife in child-bed, the first year. He is the very

---

14   Newton had previously met Whitefield in London.

15   'Mr. M.' is Martin Madan (1726-1790), a Calvinist Methodist preacher closely associated with the Countess of Huntington. He published numerous works, including a popular *A Collection of Psalms and Hymns*. 'Madan, Martin (1726-1790)', *Dictionary of National Biography*, Vol. XXXV. New York: Macmillan & Co., 1893, 288-290.

picture of sorrow. I attempt to comfort him, though I succeed but poorly. It is only God who can [give] comfort, in such a case. Yet I think few can be more capable of sympathizing with him, than myself. [What] I have lately gone through, is fresh upon my mind.[16] And why was not the event the same to me? Every [way] I am distinguished [i.e. privileged].

My prayers turn much upon the thoughts of our future settlement. It will require much prudence and resolution, to set out right at the first; but if we ask of God, it shall be given us. I would have you gradually prepare our sister, for such a house as it will be our duty, and privilege to keep, where God may be worshipped, and nothing practiced or permitted, that is contrary to our Christian profession.

By October Mary was able to make the journey to Liverpool, and the Newtons remained together throughout the stay at Liverpool. There was little evangelical preaching in Liverpool, and the Newtons sought out good pastors in nearby areas. John himself began to be called upon to preach. His first sermons were not too successful, but friends continued to encourage him. In December, 1758, John applied to preach to the Bishop of Chester and again had to be separated from Mary.

Warrington, December 13 [1758]

My dearest, ...

Now and then I feel some twinges at being forced from you, but for a season, but the cause makes amends. Three or four weeks will, I hope, re-unite us; and then, one hour will repay the pains of absence. Let us not wish away the interval, but make the most of it, then it will soon be over. The new scene of life which appears to be opening before us, is very important. We have need to pray earnestly, constantly, for each other, and for ourselves. Make much of the means of grace, reserve seasons for retirement. Endeavour to avoid the

---

16   Newton refers here to Mary's serious illness during which she was near death.

company by which you cannot improve, and to improve by that which you cannot avoid. Adieu. May the peace of God here, prepare you for his glory hereafter. Amen!

Newton was refused permission to preach because he had never been to a university and had Methodist acquaintances. John was ready to become a Dissenter (not part of the established Church of England), but Mary encouraged him to wait for the Lord's time.

Continuing as Tide Collector, Newton was sometimes away from home, or Mary went away to visit her family. When separated even briefly, John's thoughts were of Mary, and he would write to her. His letters continued to reveal his spiritual concerns - one of which was that his love for Mary was so great (after ten years of marriage) that it bordered on idolatry. He always wanted them to find their greatest love in the Lord.

> Hunslett, 17 May [1759]
> I cannot tell you how often your dear name has been in my mouth, since I left you, nor how earnestly, and frequently, I commend you to the Lord's blessing. May he teach us to improve these short, occasional separations. When I am absent from you, I most sensibly feel how dear you are to me; and what a heavy trial I should have, if God was to take you wholly from me. I ought to believe, that He will enable me to bear, whatever he may appoint, because such is his promise; but at present, it seems, that a blow so near to my heart, would be long, and deeply felt, in every other circumstance of life, and that I should find pleasure in nothing, but in bemoaning my loss. I doubt not, but you have similar thoughts, upon the supposition of my being removed. May we therefore learn, in the first place, to be thankful that we have been so often restored, and so long preserved, to each other, and that our affection is still maintained inviolable, and increasing. And secondly, to be watchful and cautious, that we do not, by our idolatry, or

ingratitude, render it necessary for the Lord, even in mercy, to wound us in the most sensible part, and to punish either of us, in the person of the other.

London July 4 [1760]

You did not bid me write, because I suppose you hardly thought I could refrain for so many tedious days, from giving my mind a little vent. How often have I told you, that whatever pleasure or amusement, I may find in the company of friends, yet there is a peculiar something that shares in, and gives an inexpressible cast to, every motion of my mind, when you are absent? A man deprived of his right hand, may go about his business with the same spirit and alacrity, as in time past, yet everything he undertakes, will necessarily remind, and convince him of his loss. This, or something like it, I may have hinted a thousand times; but as I write and speak from my heart, the thought occurs as readily to me, as at the first, and I cannot easily avoid repeating it. I am afraid of idolatry, I am afraid we have been, and still are, too guilty of the charge; and the Lord to whom alone we belong, and to whom all our services and affections are primarily due, might justly, very justly blast our boasted paradise. Yet we owe to him that our souls are susceptive of tender, and generous feelings. He formed us for each other, and his good Providence brought us together. It is no wonder if so many years, so many endearments, so many obligations, have produced an uncommon effect; and that by long habit, it is become almost impossible for me to draw a breath, of which you are not concerned. If this mutual affection leads us to this fountain from which our blessings flow, and if we can regard each other, and everything about us, with a reference to that eternity to which we are hasting, then we are happy indeed. Then not even death (the dread of mortals, especially of those who live in the possession of their wishes) can greatly harm us. Death itself can only part us for a little space, as the pier of a bridge, divides the stream for a few moments but cannot make a real separation ... methinks a regard like ours is designed to flourish in a better world than this, and can never be displayed to its full extent, and advantage, until transplanted into those regions of light and joy, where all that is imperfect, and transient, shall be no more known. Here then is the true plan of happiness for us; to consider that God who made us, made us immortals; and appointed us to spend so many years in the most interesting connection, not only to sweeten the cares of life, and to render our path through the wilderness more easy; but chiefly, that we might be helpful in animating each other, in our progress to that kingdom and crown, which is incorruptible and undefiled -- a kingdom to which we are called by Him, who died once, to give us right, and now lives for ever, to give us entrance.

Newton went to London to interview the Bishop of Chester again about becoming a priest in the Church of England. The Bishop was not encouraging until Newton produced a letter from the second Earl of Dartmouth offering Newton the curacy of the parish church of Olney in Buckinghamshire. Dartmouth was an evangelical and had been very impressed with a published account of Newton's early life. The Bishop of Chester turned very favorable to Newton once he read Dartmouth's letter.

London, 5 April [1764]

Your poor husband has need of your prayers, that he may not forget himself, amidst the many cares he meets with. I hope I shall not, but my heart is deceitful, and desperately wicked; and I can already see how prosperity blinds, and hurts, even persons of good sense, and much experience. I cannot but be pleased to find so many gracious people, in the higher scale of life. But I hope I could take as much pleasure in conversing with the poor of the flock. I think

I should be happy at Olney, if the Lord made me useful to the people there, though neither they, nor I, should be spoken of, beyond the bounds of the parish. I am glad you are pleased with the prospect; for no earthly consideration can animate me so much as to have our hearts, and desires united in this point, as they are in every thing else. What a blessing do I possess in our undivided, unabated affection! May the Lord sanctify it, as a mean to lead us both more closely to himself. We are comparatively happy now; but we shall not be completely so, till we arrive in the better world of perfect peace and purity. My heart rejoices at the thought of meeting you at Liverpool; but what will that be, to the joy, when we shall stand together before the throne of glory, free from every imperfection and trial; when we shall see Jesus as he is; be fully conformed to his image, and join in singing his praises forever . With what complacence shall I then consider you, as the instrument the Lord prepared, to preserve me from ruin? And how will you praise him for our union, if he is pleased to make me in any measure useful, to promote your faith and hope!

I cannot as yet judge, how my affairs will terminate. If it please the Lord; if it be the right place, and the right time, I shall succeed. But I would have you prepared, for what we call, a disappointment. But disappointments, are neither more nor less, than providential intimations of the will of God.

Buckden, 28 April [1764]

I have waited upon the bishop, this afternoon; have gone through all the previous form, and am to be ordained (if the Lord please) at eleven tomorrow.

I hope the repeated intimations I have given you, concerning this long-expected tomorrow, have been in time to engage you in constant prayer for me. I near almost stagger at the prospect before me. My heart is, in some measure, though

I dare not say suitably, affected. I am to stand in a very public point of view, to take the charge of a large parish; to answer the incessant demands of stated, and occasional services; to preach what I ought, and to be what I preach. Oh! what zeal, faith, patience, watchfulness, and courage will be needful for my support and guidance! My only hope is in the name, and power of Jesus. May that precious name be as ointment poured forth, to your soul and mine! May that power be triumphantly manifested in our weakness! I purpose now, to cross the country to Olney, just to stop at the place, and people, and to take the Liverpool coach, at Stony Stratford. If so, we may meet on Thursday. My heart jumps at the thought. But the Lord's time will be best.

Newton moved to the little market town of Olney in May. Mary was ill at Chatham and was unable to join John until the end of summer. Olney was one of the poorest towns in England, with lace-making and farming its main occupations.

Olney, 14 July [1764]

I observe what you say about Hampstead.[17] It seems a situation in some respects desirable, and was I only to consult my affection for you, I should wish to see you in more agreeable circumstances, than I can expect to procure you here. But we have striking examples, to remind us of the danger of choosing for ourselves, and being dazzled by great prospects. I am well convinced, that the Lord brought us hither, and without as clear an intimation of his will, I hope we shall not indulge a wish for a removal. ...

Olney, 5 August [1764]

... If I consider the endearing union he has cemented between us, with all its effects, only in a temporal view,

---

17   Shortly after he settled in Olney, some of John's friends suggested he become minister of the wealthier church in Hampstead near London. The increased wealth did not tempt John away from his sense of clear calling to Olney.

I prefer it to all the treasures, pleasures, and honours, this world can afford. So that I would not exchange the joy I feel, in the thought that you are mine, to the monarch of the whole earth. But surely it is much more valuable, considered as the mean, by which the Lord designed to unite us both to himself.

After she moved to Olney, Mary sometimes left John in Olney while she went to visit family and friends. Letters kept them in touch during these times of separation.

Olney, 12 September [1766]

I pray God to bless you, the ordinances and conversation you are favoured with in London, that you may go into Kent,[18] filled with the spirit of truth and love. When you are there I hope you will make good use of the bible, and throne of grace, to preserve you from being infected by the spirit of the world. Ah! what a poor vain thing is the world! We have both found it so at times, (though we once loved it) and shall find it so again. But may the Lord keep us alive to a sense of its vanity before more evil days return to extort the confession from our feelings. Sickness and pain, and a near prospect of death, force upon the mind a conviction of the bitterness and vanity of a worldly life. But there is a more pleasing way of learning this lesson, if we pay due attention to the word of God, and pray for the light of his countenance. If he is pleased to make his face shine upon us, all that the world can offer to bribe us, will appear insignificant and trivial, as the sports of children.

... Let us then excite each other to praise him! I hope this little interval of absence will be useful, to make me more sensible of his goodness, in still sparing you to me. I make but a poor shift without you now, from day to day, but I am

---

18   Mary's hometown of Chatham was in Kent near London.

comforted by the hope of seeing you again shortly. Had you been released by your late fever, I should not have had this relief! May we then live to him, and may every day be a preparation for the parting hour. Dark as this hour seems at the prospect, if we are established in the faith and hope of our Lord, we shall find it supportable; and the separation will be short. We shall soon meet again. Happy meeting! To part no more! To be for ever with the Lord. To join in an eternal song, to him who loved us, and washed us from our sins, in his own blood! Then all tears shall be wiped from our eyes, and we shall weep no more for ever.

Olney, 5 May [1768]

Your last dear letter found me in peace, and I hope, did me good. It quickened my prayers and praises on your behalf. I never attempt to pray, without putting up some petitions for your spiritual welfare, nor without aiming, at least to express my sense of gratitude to the Lord, for joining our hands and hearts. Your affection, and its consequences, are continually upon my mind, and I feel you in almost every thought. I am writing to hope, that I am, in some degree, freed from the idolatrous regard, which made me place you too long in a light, for which I deserved to forfeit you every day. But I am sure my love has suffered no abatement; yea, I am sure it has increased from year to year; though I endeavour to hold you in more subordination to him, to whom I owe you, and by whose blessing alone it is, that we have found comfort in each other. I trust the Lord had a further design than our accommodation in the present life, in bringing us together; even that we might be joint witnesses and partakers of his grace, and fellow-heirs of his salvation. Our earthly connection must cease; but, an eternal union in happiness, is an important prospect indeed! Everything else, however valuable in its place, sinks into nothing, upon the comparison. ...

... if we are united in the faith, and hope of the gospel, we shall never part. Even that separation which must take place (so painful at times to think of) will not deserve the name of parting. It will be but like the one coming down from London, and the other safely following in a few days.

Olney, 26 November [1775]

I am thinking of you and lifting up my heart for you, almost continually. You are in the Lord's school. He sent you, to give you the most satisfactory proofs, of his goodness to your father; which, I hope, will prove an encouragement, and a cause of great thankfulness to yourself.[19] He is very gracious, and I trust, will shew himself so to you, and in you. But you deprive yourself of comfort, by listening to the voice of unbelief; which weakens your hands, and prevents your progress. How often are you distressed, as though you were only to see, the goodness of the Lord to others, and not to taste of it yourself! Yet the path of few peoples through life, has been more marked with peculiar mercies than yours. How differently has he led us from the way we should have chosen for ourselves! We have had remarkable turns in our affairs; but every change has been for the better; and in every trouble (for we have had our troubles) he has given us effectual help. Shall we not then believe, that he will perfect that which concerns us? When I was an infant, and knew not what I wanted, he sent you into the world to be, first, the principal hinge, upon which my part, and character in life, was to turn and then to be my companion. We have traveled together near twenty-six years; and though we are changeable creatures, and have seen almost every thing change around us, he has preserved our affections, by his blessings, or we might have been weary

---

19   Mary's father was ailing at Chatham, and she had gone to bring him back to Olney to live in the vicarage with them. He died there just over a year later.

of each other. How far we have yet to go, we know not; but the greater, and (as to externals) the pleasanter part of our journey is, probably passed over. If our lives are prolonged, the shadows of the evening, old age, with its attendant infirmities, will be pressing upon us soon. Yet I hope this uncertain remaining part of our pilgrimage, will upon the whole, be the best: for our God is all-sufficient, and can make us more happy, by the light of his countenance, when our temporal comforts fail, than we ever were, when we possessed them to the greatest advantage.

At the end of 1779, the Newtons left Olney for John to become rector at St. Mary Woolnoth's in London. There he ministered for the next quarter century.

Mary died on December 15, 1790, after a long illness. Newton was by her side and later wrote:

> When I was sure she was gone, I took off her ring, according to her repeated injunction, and put it upon my own finger. I then kneeled down, with the servants who were in the room, and returned the Lord my unfeigned thanks for her deliverance, and her peaceful dismission.
>
> How wonderful must be the moment after death! What a transition did she then experience! She was instantly freed from sin, and all its attendant sorrows, and I trust, instantly admitted to join the heavenly choir. That moment, was remarkable to me, likewise. It removed from me, the chief object, which made another day, or hour of life, as to my own personal concern, desirable. ...

Newton realized that as a minister he must suffer affliction as an example to fellow Christians, and he continued to preach throughout Mary's illness. He preached her funeral sermon:

> I was not supported by lively, sensible considerations, but by being enabled to realize to my mind, some great and leading

truths to the word of God. I saw, what indeed I knew before, but never till then so strongly and clearly perceived, that as a sinner, I had no right, and as a believer, I could have no reason, to complain. I considered her as a loan, which He who lent her to me, had a right to resume whenever He pleased; and that as I had deserved to forfeit her every day, from the first; it became me, rather to be thankful that she was spared to me so long. ...

When my wife died, the world seemed to die with her, (I hope, to revive no more). I see little now, but my ministry and my Christian profession, to make a continuance in life, for a single day, desirable; though I am willing to wait my appointed time.[20]

John himself died December 21, 1807. He wrote his own epitaph, which can still be read in St. Mary Woolnoth's:

JOHN NEWTON
CLERK
ONCE AN INFIDEL AND LIBERTINE,
A SERVANT OF SLAVES IN AFRICA,
WAS, BY THE RICH MERCY OF OUR LORD AND SAVIOUR
JESUS CHRIST,
PRESERVED, RESTORED, PARDONED,
AND APPOINTED TO PREACH THE FAITH
HE HAD LONG LABOURED TO DESTROY.

HE MINISTERED
NEAR XVI YEARS AS CURATE AND VICAR OF *OLNEY* IN
BUCKS
AND XXVIII AS RECTOR
OF THESE UNITED PARISHES.

ON FEBRY THE FIRST MDCCL HE MARRIED
MARY
DAUGHTER OF THE LATE GEORGE CATLETT,
OF *CHATHAM KENT,*

---

20   Newton included an account of Mary's death as an appendix in his *Letters to a Wife.*

WHOM HE RESIGNED
TO THE LORD WHO GAVE HER, ON
DECR THE XVTH MDCCXC.

John always recognized Mary's love as part of God's Amazing Grace.

CHARLES H. SPURGEON
AND
SUSANNAH SPURGEON

(1834-1892)   (1832-1903)

'None know how grateful I am to God for you. In all I have ever done for Him, you have a large share, for in making me so happy, you have fitted me for service.'

Charles Spurgeon

While attending the brilliant opening of London's Crystal Palace June 20, 1854, Charles Spurgeon read Susannah Thompson these lines from Martin Tupper's *Proverbial Philosophy*:

> Seek a good wife of thy God, for she is the best gift of His providence,
> Yet ask not in bold confidence that which He has not promised.
> Thou knowest not His good will; be thy prayer then submissive thereunto,
> And leave thy petition to His mercy, assured that he will deal well with thee.
> If thou art to have a wife of thy youth, she is now living on the earth;
> Therefore think of her, and pray for her weal.[1]

---

1   Martin Farquhar Tupper. *Proverbial Philosophy*. New York and Auburn: Miller, Orton, and Mulligan, 1856, p. 113.

He then asked her in a soft voice, 'Do you pray for him who is to be your husband?' Susannah's heart raced, her eyes fell, and she blushed at the young pastor's words. After the opening ceremonies, the young couple walked together through the Crystal Palace, the gardens, and down to the lake. Susannah wrote years later, 'During that walk, in that memorable day in June, I believe God Himself united our hearts in indissoluble bonds of true affection, and though we knew it not, gave us to each other for ever.'[2]

Though Spurgeon would become the most popular preacher of the nineteenth century, Susannah had not been impressed with him at all when she first saw and heard him. She was present December 18, 1853, the Sunday the nineteen-year-old Spurgeon first preached at New Park Street Church, 'So this is his so-called eloquence! It does not impress me. What a painful countrified manner! Will he ever quit making flourishes with that terrible blue silk handkerchief! And his hair - why, he looks like a barber's assistant!'[3]

Yet, Susannah came to know Christ and grow under Spurgeon's teaching and ministry. When Susannah was concerned about her spiritual state, Charles sent her a copy of Bunyan's *Pilgrim's Progress*, inscribed, 'Miss Thompson, with desires for her progress in the blessed pilgrimage, from C.H. Spurgeon.' One of her first gifts to him was a complete set of the writings of John Calvin. In later years Spurgeon wrote in the first volume:

> The volumes making up a complete set of Calvin were a gift to me from my own most dear, and tender wife. Blessed may she be among women. How much of comfort and strength she has ministered unto me it is not in my power to estimate. She has been to me God's best earthly gift, and not a little even of heavenly treasure has come to me by her means. She has often been as an angel of God unto me.[4]

2   *The Autobiography of Charles H. Spurgeon*, compiled by his wife and private secretary. Philadelphia: American Baptist Publication Society, n.d., Vol. II, 11.

3   Richard Ellsworth Day, *The Shadow of the Broad Brim*. Valley Forge: The Judson Press, 1965, 107.

4   *Autobiography*, Vol. II, 11.

On August 2, 1854, Charles and Susannah declared their love for each other in her grandfather's garden. Susannah later wrote that with great awe

> ... [I] left my beloved, and hastening to the house and to an upper room, I knelt before God, and praised and thanked him, with happy tears, for His great mercy in giving me the love of so good a man. If I had known, then, how good he was, and how great he would become, I would have been overwhelmed, not so much with the happiness of being his, as with responsibility which such a position would entail.

In her diary that evening, Susannah wrote, 'It is impossible to write down all that occurred this morning. I can only adore in silence the mercy of my God, and praise Him for all His benefits.'[5]

During their courtship, Charles and Susannah developed a kinship in spiritual things which only deepened in married life. They spent time reading together Jonathan Edwards, Richard Baxter, and other old Puritan writers. Together they published a collection of Puritan theology called *Smooth Stones Taken from Ancient Brooks*. Personal conversion was an important part of Puritan theology, and preparatory to Spurgeon baptizing Susannah in February, 1855, he asked her to write out her personal testimony of her conversion. In his letter to Susannah on January 11, Spurgeon expressed his satisfaction with Susannah's spiritual depth.

75, Dover Road[6]

January 11, 1855

My Dearest,

The letter is all I can desire. Oh! I could weep for joy (as I certainly am doing now) to think that my beloved can so well testify to a work of grace in her soul. I knew you were

---

5   *Autobiography*, Vol. II, 9.

6   Unless otherwise noted, all letters of Spurgeon's are from *The Autobiography of Charles H. Spurgeon*, compiled from his diary, letters, and records by his wife and private secretary. Philadelphia: American Baptist Publication Society, n.d. 75, Dover Road was Spurgeon's address in London.

really a child of God, but I did not think you had been led in such a path. I see my Master has been ploughing deep, and it is the deep-sown seed, struggling with the clods, which now makes your bosom heave with distress. If I know anything of spiritual symptoms, I think I know a cure for you. Your position is not the sphere for earnest labour for Christ. You have done all you could in more ways than one; but you are not brought into actual contact either with the saints, or with the sinful, sick, or miserable, whom you could serve. Active service brings with it warmth, and this tends to remove doubting, for our works thus become evidences of our calling and election.

I flatter no one, but allow me to say, honestly, that few cases which have come under my notice are so satisfactory as yours. Mark, I write not now as your *admiring friend*, but impartially as your Pastor. If the Lord had intended your destruction, He would not have told you such things as these, nor would He enable you so unreservedly to cast yourself upon His faithful promise. As I hope to stand at the bar of God, clear of the blood of all men, it would ill become me to flatter; and as I love you with the deepest and purest affection, far be it from me to trifle with your immortal interests; but I will say again that my gratitude to God ought to be great, as well on my own behalf as yours, that you have been so deeply schooled in the lessons of the heart, and have so frequently looked into the charnel-house of your own corruption. There are other lessons to come, that you may be thoroughly furnished; but oh! my dear one, how good to learn the first lesson well! I loved you once, but feared you might not be an heir of Heaven; - God in His mercy showed me that you were indeed *elect*. I then thought I might without sin reveal my affection to you, - but up to the time I saw your note, I could not imagine that you had seen such great sights, and were so thoroughly versed in soul-knowledge. God is good, very good, infinitely good. Oh, how I prize this last gift, because I now know, more than ever, that the Giver loves the gift, and so I may love it, too, but only in subservience to Him. Dear purchase of a Saviour's blood, you are to me a Saviour's gift, and my heart is full to overflowing with the thought of such continued goodness. I do not wonder at His goodness, for it is just like Him; but I cannot but lift up the voice of joy at His manifold mercies.

Whatever befall us, trouble and adversity, sickness or death, we need not fear a final separation, either from each other, or our God. I am glad you are not here just at this moment, for I feel so deeply that I could only throw my arms around you and weep. May the choicest favours be thine, may the Angel of the Covenant be thy companion, may thy supplications be answered, and may thy conversation be with Jesus in Heaven! Farewell; unto my God and my father's God I commend you.

Yours, with pure and holy affection, as well as terrestrial love,

C.H. Spurgeon

In the spring, Spurgeon took Susie to meet his parents in Colchester. After spending a few days together there with Spurgeon's family, the couple returned to their homes in London. Spurgeon wrote Susie the following Friday.

75, Dover Road,
April, '55.

My Own Doubly-dear Susie,

How much we have enjoyed in each other's society! It seems almost impossible that I could either have conferred or received so much happiness. I feel now, like you, very low in spirits; but a sweet promise in Ezekiel cheers me, 'I will give thee the opening of the mouth in the midst of them."[7] Surely my God has not forgotten me. Pray for me, my love; and may our united petitions win a blessing through the Saviour's merit! Let us take heed of putting ourselves too prominently in our own hearts, but let us commit our way unto the Lord. 'What I have in my own hand, I usually lose,' said Luther; 'but what I put into God's hand, is still, and ever will be, in my possession.' I need not send my love to you, for, though absent in body, my heart is with you still, and I am, your much-loved, and ardently loving, C.H.S.

P.S.-The devil has barked again in *The Essex Standard.*[8] It contains another letter. Never mind; when Satan opens his mouth, he gives me an opportunity of ramming my sword down his throat.

St. Ann's Terrace,[9]

April, '55

My Dearest,

I thank you with warm and hearty thanks for the note just received. It is useless for me to attempt to tell you how much happiness I have had during the past week. Words are but cold dishes on which to serve up thoughts and feelings which come warm and glowing from the heart. I should like to express my appreciations of all the tenderness and care you have shown towards me during this happy week; but I fear to pain you by thanks for what I know was a pleasure

---

7   Ezekiel 29:21.

8   Attacks on Spurgon's ministry began only a few months after he became pastor of the Park Street Church. Other pastors even wrote articles in magazines and newspapers questioning his conversion, warning that his teaching was a mixture of truth and error, and attacking his dramatic style of preaching. One article, entitled 'A Clerical Poltroon' said, 'All his discourses are redolent of bad taste, are vulgar and theatrical, an insult to God and man' (John Woodbridge, ed. *More Than Conquerors*. Chicago: Moody Bible Institute, 1992, 198). Though Spurgeon was deeply hurt by such attacks, he never replied to them and went about his ministry.

9   Susannah was living with her parents and her uncle.

to you. I expect your thoughts have been busy to-day about the 'crown Jewels' [a sermon he was preparing]. The gems may differ in size, colour, richness, and beauty, but even the smallest are 'precious stones,' are they not?

That *Standard* certainly does not bear 'Excelsior' as its motto; nor can 'Good will to men' be the device of its floating pennon[10], but it matters not; we *know* that all is under the control of One of whom Asaph said, 'Surely the wrath of man shall praise Thee; the remainder of wrath shalt Thou restrain."[11] May His blessing rest in an especial manner on you to-night, my dearly beloved; and on the approaching Sabbath, when you stand before the great congregation, may you be 'filled with all the fulness of God!' Good-night. Fondly and faithfully yours, -Susie.

In July, Spurgeon went to Scotland, combining preaching engagements with a needed rest. In later years when Susie published some of Spurgeon's letters from this period she wrote:

I have been trying in these pages to leave the 'love' out of the letters as much as possible, lest my precious things should appear but platitudes to my readers, but it is a difficult task; for little rills of tenderness run between all the sentences, like the singing, dancing waters among the boulders of a brook, and I cannot still the music altogether. To the end of his beautiful life it was the same, his letters were always those of a devoted lover, as well as of a tender husband; not only did the brook never dry up, but the stream grew deeper and broader, and the rhythm of its song waxed sweeter and stronger.[12]

---

10   A 'pennon' was a flag or banner, usually tapering, triangular or swallow-tailed in shape.

11   Psalm 76:10.

12   *Autobiography*, Vol. II, 23-24.

Aberfeldy
July 17th, 1855

My Precious Love,

Your dearly-prized note came safely to hand, and verily it did excel all I have ever read, even from your own loving pen. Well, I am all right now. Last Sabbath, I preached twice; and to sum up all in a word, the services were 'glorious.' In the morning Dr. Patterson's place was crammed; and in the evening, Dr. Wardlaw's Chapel was crowded to suffocation by more than 2,500 people, while persons outside declared that quite as many went away. My reception was enthusiastic; never was greater honour given to mortal man. They were just as delighted as were the people at Park Street. Today, I have had a fine drive with my host and his daughter. To-morrow I am to preach *here*. It is quite impossible for me to be left in quiet. Already, letters come in, begging me to go here, there, and everywhere. Unless I go to the North Pole, I never can get away from my holy labour.

Now to return to you again, I have had day-dreams of you while driving along, I thought you were very near me. It is not long, dearest, before I shall again enjoy your sweet society, if the providence of God permit. I knew I loved you very much before, but now I feel how necessary you are to me; and you will not lose much by my absence, if you find me, on my return, more attentive to your feelings as equally affectionate. I can now thoroughly sympathize with your tears, because I feel in no little degree that pang of absence which my constant engagements prevented me from noticing when in London. How then must you, with so much leisure, have felt my absence from you, even though you well knew that it was unavoidable on my part! My darling, accept love of the deepest and purest kind from one who is not prone to exaggerate, but who feels that here there is no room for hyperbole. Think not that I weary myself by writing; for, my dearest, it is my delight to please you, and solace an absence which must be even more dreary to you than to me, since traveling and preaching lead me to forget it. My eyes ache for sleep, but they shall keep open till I have invoked the blessings from above - mercies temporal and eternal - to rest on the head of one whose name is sweet to me, and who equally loves the name of her own, her much-loved, C.H.S.

Great crowds followed Spurgeon's preaching tour in Scotland, and he was deeply aware of the dangers of being exalted by pride or departing from the Lord because of his success. He asked Susie for her prayers.

[1855, during preaching tour of Scotland] I shall feel deeply indebted to you, if you will pray very earnestly for me. I fear I am not so full of love to God as I used to be. I lament my sad decline in spiritual things. You and others may not have observed it, but I am now conscious of it, and a sense thereof has put bitterness in my cup of joy. Oh! what is it to be popular, to be successful, to have abundance, even to have love so sweet as yours, - if I should be left of God to fall, and to depart from His ways? I tremble at the giddy height on which I stand, and could wish myself unknown, for indeed I am unworthy of all my honours and fame. I trust I shall now commence anew, and wear no longer the linsey-woolsey garment; but I beseech you, blend your hearty prayers with mine, that two of us may be agreed, and thus will you promote the usefulness, and holiness, and happiness of one whom you love.

Spurgeon spent the last Christmas before his marriage with his parents in Colchester.

[Colchester, December, 1855]

Sweet One, -

How I love you! I long to see you; and yet it is but half-an-hour since I left you. Comfort yourself in my absence by the thought that my heart is with you. My own gracious God bless you in all things, - in heart, in feeling, in life, in death, in Heaven! May your virtues be perfected, your prospects realized, your zeal continued, your love in Him increased, and your knowledge of Him rendered deeper, higher, broader, - in fact, may more than even *my heart* can wish, or *my* hope anticipate, be yours forever! May we be mutual blessings; -wherein I shall err, you will pardon; and wherein you may mistake, I will more than overlook. Yours, till Heaven, *and then,* - C.H.S.

Charles and Susannah Spurgeon were married January 9, 1856. Their love grew in the ensuing years; the many trials and troubles each faced only strengthened their spiritual oneness. By the time he was thirty, Spurgeon suffered from gout and its accompanying depression. Susie also was ill and did not leave the house for fifteen years. Yet each was the greatest support of the other, and their spiritual bond deepened their love.

In 1865, while on an evangelistic trip, Spurgeon wrote for Susie some verses expressing his love for her:

Married Love - To my wife

by C.H. Spurgeon

Over the space which parts us, my wife,
I'll cast me a bridge of song.
Our hearts shall meet, O joy of my life,
On its arch unseen but strong.

As the river never forgets the sea,
But hastes to the ocean's breast,
My constant soul flows onward to thee,
And finds in thy love its rest.

The swallows must plume their wings to greet
New summers in lands afar;
But dwelling at home with thee I meet
No winter my year to mar.

The wooer his new love's name may wear
Engraved on a precious stone;
But in my heart thine image I wear,
That heart has been long thine own.

The glowing colours on surface laid,
Wash out in a shower of rain,
Thou need'st not be of rivers afraid,
For my love is dyed ingrain.

And as ev'ry drop of Gonda's lake
Is tinged with the sapphire's blue.
So all the joys of my mind partake
Of joy at the thought of you.

The glittering dewdrops of dawning love
Exhale as the day grows old,
And fondness, taking the wings of a dove,
Is gone like a vale of old,

But mine for thee, from the chambers of joy,
With strength came forth as the sun;
Nor life nor death shall its force destroy,
For ever its course shall run.

All earthborn love must sleep in the grave,
To its nature dust return;
What God hath kindled shall death outbrave,
And in Heav'n itself shall burn.

Beyond and above the wedlock tie
Our union to Christ we feel,
Uniting bonds which were made on high
Shall hold us when earth shall reel.

> Though He who chose us all worlds before,
> Must <u>reign</u> in our hearts alone,
> We fondly believe that we shall adore
> <u>Together</u> before His throne.[13]

Other letters reveal the Spurgeons' continuing love throughout their lives.

[1871]

My Own Dear One, --None know how grateful I am to God for you. In all I have ever done for Him, you have a large share, for in making me so happy you have fitted me for service. Not an ounce of power has ever been lost to the good cause through you. I have served the Lord far more, and never less, for your sweet companionship. The Lord God Almighty bless you now and forever!

[1871]

I have been thinking over my strange history, and musing on eternal love's great river-head from which such streams of mercy have flowed to me. I dwell devoutly on many points; --the building of the Tabernacle,-- what a business it was, and how little it seems now! Do you remember a Miss Thompson who collected for the enlargement of the New Park Street Chapel as much as £100? Bless her dear heart! Think of the love which gave me that dear lady for a wife, and made her such a wife; to me, the ideal wife, and, as I believe, without exaggeration or love-flourishing, the precise form in which God would make a woman for such a man as I am, if He designed her to be the greatest of all earthly blessings to him; and in some sense a spiritual blessing, too, for in that also am I richly profited by you, though you would not believe it. I will leave this 'good matter' ere the paper is covered; but not till I have sent you as many kisses as there are waves on the sea.

---

13 *Autobiography*, Vol. II, 298-299.

[Undated][14]

MY OWN DEAR SUFFERER,-

I am pained indeed to learn, from T__'s kind note, that you are still in so sad a condition! Oh, may the ever-merciful God be pleased to give you ease!

I have been quite a long round to-day, if a 'round' can be 'long.' First, to Finsbury, to buy the wardrobe, - a beauty. I hope you will live long to hang your garments in it, every thread of them precious to me for your dear sake. Next, to Hewlett's, for a chandelier for the dining room. Found one quite to my taste and yours. Then to Negretti & Zambra's, to buy a barometer for my very own fancy, for I have promised to treat myself to one. On the road, I obtained the Presburg biscuits, and within their box I send this note, hoping it may reach you the more quickly. They are sweetened with my love and prayers.

The bedroom will look well with the wardrobe in it; at least, so I hope. It is well made; and, I believe, as nearly as I could tell, precisely all you wished for. Joe (Mr. Passmore gave this handsome present) is very good, and should have a wee note whenever darling feels she could write it without too much fatigue; - but not yet. I bought also a table for you in case you should have to keep your bed. It rises or falls by a screw, and also winds sideways, so as to go over the bed, and then it has a flap for a book or paper, so that my dear one may read or write in comfort while lying down. I could not resist the pleasure of making this little gift to my poor suffering wifey, only hoping it might not often be in requisition, but might be a help when there was a needs-be for it. Remember, all I buy, I pay for. I have paid for everything as yet with the earnings of my pen, graciously sent me in time of need. It is my ambition to leave nothing

---

14   *The Letters of C.H. Spurgeon*, collected by his son Charles Spurgeon. London: Marshall Brothers, 1923.

for you to be anxious about. I shall find the money for the curtains, etc., and you will amuse yourself by giving orders for them after your own delightful taste.

I must not write more; and, indeed, matter runs short except the old, old story of a love which grieves over you, and would fain work a miracle, and raise you up to perfect health. I fear the heat afflicts you. Well did the elder say to John in Patmos, concerning those who are before the throne of God, 'neither shall the sun light on them, nor any heat.'[15]

Yours to love in life, and death, and eternally,

C.H.S.

Spurgeon's description of a happy marriage and the true wife actually describes his beloved Susie:

Sometimes we have seen a model marriage, founded on pure love, and cemented in mutual esteem. Therein, the husband acts as a tender head; and the wife, as a true spouse, realizes the model marriage-relation, and sets forth what our oneness with the Lord ought to be. She delights in her husband, in his person, his character, his affection; to her, he is not only the chief and foremost of mankind, but in her eyes he is all-in-all; her heart's love belongs to him, and to him only. She finds sweetest content and solace in his company, his fellowship, his fondness; he is her little world, her Paradise, her choice treasure. At any time, she would gladly lay aside her own pleasure to find it doubled in gratifying him. She is glad to sink her individuality in his. She seeks no renown for herself; his honour is reflected upon her, and she rejoices in it. She would defend his name with her dying breath; safe enough is he where she can speak for him. The domestic circle is her kingdom; that she may there create happiness and comfort, is her life-work; and his smiling gratitude is

---

15   Revelation 7:16.

all the reward she seeks. Even in her dress, she thinks of him; without constraint she consults his taste and considers nothing beautiful which is distasteful to him. A tear from his eye, because of any unkindness on her part, would grievously torment her. She asks not how her behaviour may please a stranger, or how another's judgment may approve her conduct; let her beloved be content, and she is glad. He has many objects in life, some of which she does not quite understand; but she believes in them all, and anything she can do to promote them, she delights to perform. He lavishes love on her, and, in return, she lavishes love on him. Their object in life is common. There are points where their affections so intimately unite that none could tell which is first and which is second. To watch their children growing up in health and strength, to see them holding posts of usefulness and honour, is their mutual concern; in this and other matters, they are fully one. Their wishes blend, their hearts are indivisible. By degrees, they come to think very much the same thoughts. Intimate association creates conformity; I have known this to become so complete that, at the same moment, the same utterance has leaped to both their lips.

Happy woman and happy man! If Heaven be found on earth, they have it! At last, the two are so blended, so engrafted on one stem, that their old age presents a lovely attachment, a common sympathy, by which its infirmities are greatly alleviated, and its burdens are transformed into fresh bonds of love. So happy a union of will, sentiment, thought, and heart exists between them, that the two streams of their life have washed away the dividing bank, and run on as one broad current of united existence till their common joy falls into the ocean of eternal felicity.[16]

---

16 *Autobiography*, Vol. II, 52.

After Spurgeon's death, Susannah wrote, 'for though God has seen fit to call my beloved up to higher service, He has left me the consolation of still loving him with all my heart, and believing that our love shall be perfected when we meet in that blessed land where Love reigns supreme and eternal.'[17]

---

17 *Autobiography*, Vol. II, 8.

PICTURE ACKNOWLEDGMENT

Thomas J. Jackson & Mary Anna Jackson
Memoirs of Stonewall Jackson. Louisville, Ky.: Courier-Journal Job Printing, 1895.

John Winthrop
Portrait property of the American Antiquarian Society.

Mrs Winthrop
Portrait property of the Massachusetts Historical Society. The exact identity of 'Mrs Winthrop' is unknown. This might be Margaret, or another 'Mrs Winthrop.'

Henry Martyn
Frontispiece of Henry Sargent's *The Life and Letters of Henry Martyn*, Banner of Truth Trust 1985 reprint of earlier 1862 edition.

Missionaries and Tocat memorial
In personal possession of author.

Dietrich Bonhoeffer and Maria von Wedemeyer:
Love Letters from Cell 92. HarperCollins Publishers, 1994.

Christopher Love:
Don Kistler's *A Spectacle unto God*. Soli Deo Gloria Publications, 1994.

John Newton:
Christian History & Biography, Issue 81, Winter 2004.

Charles and Susannah Spurgeon:
Bob L. Ross, *A Pictorial Biography of C.H. Spurgeon*. Pilgrim Publications, Pasadena, Texas 77501.

Other titles available...

Diana Lynn Severance

Feminine Threads

Women in the Tapestry of Christian History

ISBN 978-1-84550-640-7

Feminine Threads
Women in the Tapestry of Christian History

DIANA LYNN SEVERANCE

From commoner to queen, the women in this book embraced the freedom and the power of the Gospel in making their unique contributions to the unfolding of history. Wherever possible, the women here speak for themselves, from their letters, diaries or published works. The true story of women in Christian history inspires, challenges and demonstrates the grace of God producing much fruit throughout time.

Feminine Threads is a must-read for men and women alike, but especially so for young women who need to have a clear view of the contributions that women before them have made to the Christian faith.

Carolyn McCulley
Conference Speaker and Author of
Radical Womanhood: Feminine Faith in a Feminist World,
Arlington, Virginia

Diana Severance (phD, Rice University) is an historian with broad experience teaching in universities and seminaries.

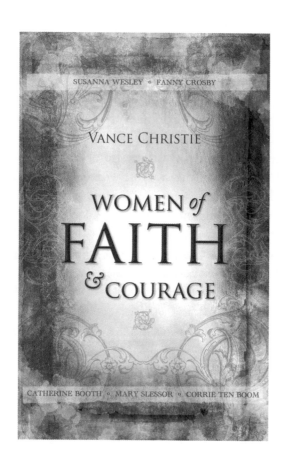

ISBN 978-1-84550-686-5